How Jesus Changes the World

Restored Dominion, the Kingdom of God, and the Gospel for Our Time

Gary C Fairchild

Copyright

ISBN: 979-8-9953552-3-6

Scripture quotations are taken from the Holy Bible, English Standard Version (ESV), unless otherwise noted.

2nd Edition

Gary C Fairchild Books, Holly Springs, NC

This work addresses historical and contemporary social issues from a theological and ethical perspective. References to political events are included for illustrative and educational purposes and are not intended as partisan advocacy.

Forewords

Dr. Timothy Crouch, Vice President of Alliance Missions, The Christian & Missionary Alliance.

"Gary Fairchild has given us a good lens for seeing the whole of the gospel's message and meaning. He gives careful attention to the Kingdom message of Jesus in Matthew and the Synoptics, and to the good news of eternal life in the Gospel of John. Then he helpfully pairs this with stories from his lifetime of observing and participating in the gospel's impact on whole lives and communities. He sharpens our focus on true dimensions of the gospel far too often blurred by forces that narrow our grasp of why the good news is so good–selfish individualism, ethnocentrism, Christian nationalism, and religious particularism. He helps us see that God is renewing the good he originally created in lives of those redeemed through Jesus, restoring dominion he intended them to have over their lives–living in harmony with God's ways, with others and with creation, beginning eternal life of his Kingdom now, on earth as it is and will be in heaven. This is the gospel experience we need and can have. And it is the gospel message we can proclaim and live for the sake of all the individuals, communities, and peoples of the world!"

Tim Undheim, PhD. seminary & graduate school professor of the Bible languages. Manila, Philippines

"As a Bible teacher in Asia and a friend of the author and his wife, I count it a privilege to be asked to write a forward to this book. In a world where the gospel is often reduced to cultural forms or entangled with political ideologies, Gary helps us return to the message of Jesus in its power and transformative impact. With plenty of examples from his personal experiences in cross cultural ministry, his emphasis on the Kingdom of God as developed in the gospels challenges us to look beyond ethnocentrism and theological exclusivism and to embrace a faith that transcends every human government and the confining grids of religious systems. The good news of Jesus is not confined to the categories of East or West; it speaks into the lives of real people, restoring dignity, peace, and grace wherever it takes root. My desire as a teacher is to help students learn not only to study the Scriptures but to live them out, reflecting God's way of compassion and justice in culturally sensitive and faithful ways. Gary's work is a true aid in that effort.

What I especially value in this book is how it highlights the restoration of lost dominion through Christ. The story of humanity is one of forfeited authority, brokenness, and fear. Yet in Jesus, God has come near to restore that which was lost—inviting us to live in grace, to steward creation wisely, and to serve one another in love. This is not a gospel of self-assertion but of renewal, not of domination but of harmony. I encourage readers to approach these pages with humility, listening as though they were among the first hearers of the gospels as they were written, for it is only when we hear the Word as it was meant for them that we can apply it faithfully in our time. My hope is that you will find in these pages both clarity and courage to live as citizens of God's Kingdom, bearing witness to the good news that indeed changes the world."

Kevin Sanderson, MBA. CAO World Relief

"How Jesus Changes the World— Community Development Perspective. Not knowing that Gary was writing this book, I was both surprised and pleased when he called a few months back to ask me to read it and write a Foreword to the book. Gary and I spent many years working together in World Relief and I have always appreciated Gary's ability to readily relate to others 'stories of transformation of families and communities always starting with the planting of the seed of the Gospel in their lives. In this book, Gary not only provides us with these stories of transformation, but he first provides us with a robust foundational understanding of why knowing and accepting Jesus 'call brings about this transformation. Using historical, geographical, cultural, and philosophical references the book provides us with a powerful, concise understanding of the Gospels and the words and life of Jesus. He then offers us a spiritual roadmap for all who long to see genuine renewal in the world around them.

Central to Gary's message from his exploration of the synoptic gospels is the understanding of the Kingdom of God as near. This nearness is not merely a proclamation of hope for the future, but an invitation to participate in the works God has placed before every believer. The "here and now" of God's Kingdom is unveiled as we engage daily in acts of kindness, justice, and restoration—each moment, ch task, a brush stroke on the larger canvas of God's redemptive plan. Community development is thus not an abstract ideal, but the very expression of the Kingdom coming alive in the homes, schools, places of work, and hearts of our neighbors.

The concept of dominion, so often misunderstood or misapplied, receives fresh consideration in this book. Theologically, dominion is not a license for exploitation but a sacred charge to steward, serve, and cultivate the flourishing of all creation. Through Jesus, we are invited into a new kind of dominion—a power that does not dominate but empowers every person, family, and community to bring about dominion over their own lives. In community development, this means harnessing the resources, talents, and passions entrusted to us, and channeling them into practical works that uplift and renew. The role of the Church in fostering this work is the power of Jesus at work, not in isolation, but with collaborative, Spirit-driven efforts helping communities seeking wholeness.

Gary's exploration of the Gospel of John brings further depth to this vision. The promise that "believing in God gives life in His name" is not merely an individual assurance, but a communal inheritance. This new life is the wellspring from which creativity, courage, and compassion flow. When we believe, we are not only transformed inwardly; we are endowed with new capabilities, a boldness to heal, to unite, to envision what our communities can become. The Gospel of John calls us to receive and share this life, lighting up the world around us with the hope, power, and possibility found in Jesus.

In considering this work through the lens of community development, we discover that when we truly embrace the teachings and acceptance of Jesus, these are not distant promises, but present realities that shape our communities, our cities, and our societies. As you read this book, you may be inspired to see your own context with new eyes.

May you grasp how the nearness of the Kingdom of God bursts forth as everyday people respond to Jesus's call doing "the good works he has set down for us to do," and how the dominion entrusted to us by Jesus is the key to unlocking transformation—not just in our personal lives, but on the streets and in the communities that people across the world call home."

Table of Contents

Introduction

Why Jesus Still Changes the World

Across history, countless books have been written about Jesus—his teachings, his miracles, his death, and his resurrection. Yet one question remains persistently relevant: What difference does Jesus actually make in the world today?

For many, faith has been reduced to private belief or future hope. Christianity is often framed as something concerned primarily with heaven, individual morality, or personal comfort. But when we return to the Gospels themselves, we encounter something far more expansive. Jesus did not simply announce forgiveness of sins or the promise of eternal life after death. He proclaimed the arrival of the Kingdom of God—a present reality that transforms how people live, relate, work, govern, and care for one another. This book is written from a conviction shaped by Scripture and experience: when people genuinely follow Jesus, lives change—and so do communities.

Over decades of pastoral ministry and international development work across Asia, Africa, Latin America, and the Middle East, I have witnessed this transformation firsthand. I have seen individuals recover dignity, families regain stability, and communities rediscover hope—not through ideology or programs alone, but through lives reshaped by the way of Jesus.

The Gospels present a unified story with diverse voices. Matthew, Mark, and Luke emphasize the Kingdom of God—God's reign breaking into human history. John, writing to a Greek audience, speaks of eternal life—not merely as life after death, but as a new quality of life available now. Together, these perspectives reveal a gospel that restores what was lost in creation: human purpose, responsibility, and stewardship—what Scripture calls dominion.

This book explores that restoration. It asks what it means to follow Jesus in everyday life, in broken systems, and in a fractured world. It connects biblical teaching with real-world implications—justice, compassion, leadership, and community renewal—without reducing the gospel to politics or sentimentality.

This is not a theoretical work. It is written for pastors, leaders, students, and thoughtful readers who want to understand how faith becomes embodied practice. It is for those who believe the message of Jesus still has the power to change the world—and want to see how.

Timeline

Ephesus inherited by Rome	B.C. 129
Death of Julius Caesar	B.C. 44
Caesar Augustus Emperor	B.C. 27
Jesus born between	B.C. 6- 4
Death of Herod the Great	B.C. 4
John the Baptist / Jesus	A.D. 30
Crucifixion & Resurrection	A.D. 33
Death of James	A.D. 44
Paul's 1st Journey	A.D.46 48
Jerusalem Council	A.D. 49
Paul's 2nd journey	A.D. 50-53
Paul's 3rd journey	A.D. 53-57
Paul's 4th journey	A.D. 57-61
Mt, Mk, Lk written	A.D. 50-70
Death of Peter and Paul	A.D. 65
Temple destroyed	A.D. 70
John arrives at Ephesus	A.D. c.87
Domitian persecution	A.D. 81-96
Death of John	A.D. 100

PART I

The Kingdom of God & The Fruit of Repentance

Matthew, Mark, and Luke

Chapter 1 The Kingdom Arrives

Genesis 1–3

In the summer of 2016, Connie and I traveled through Adirondack State Park in New York. As I drove, she read aloud from "The Hidden Life" of Trees by Peter Wohlleben. He writes of old-growth forests as places of quiet strength—ecosystems that appear almost timeless, where fallen trunks become resting places and life unfolds at a pace that calms the human spirit. Preserves where forests are allowed to mature, Wohlleben notes, offer both environmental stability and a sense of rest for those who enter them.

During that trip, we visited the Wild Center in Tupper Lake, also known as the Adirondack Natural History Museum. Inside, exhibits detailed the region's trees, plants, and wildlife. Outside, short trails led through dense forest, and an elevated walkway carried visitors into the canopy of towering trees. From that vantage point, the forest stretched for miles, rising and falling with the gentle contours of the Adirondack Mountains.

Scientists tell us that forests are essential to the survival of life on our planet. Their impact is vast, sustaining ecosystems far beyond what is visible to the casual observer.

Forests are often used as metaphors for the relationship between the global and the local, between vision and mission, between the whole and its parts. I am, by nature, a "forest" person. I am drawn to the larger picture and to understanding how a broad context gives meaning to the details of life.

Many of us grew up reading the Bible one chapter—or even one verse—at a time. We memorized passages disconnected from their wider context, yet those verses carried real power and promise. In many ways, those verses are like strong, enduring trees. Individual stories and chapters are like groves. Together, they form a living forest—the Gospel of Jesus Christ—in which individual lives find their meaning and purpose.

In this book, I want to explore the Gospel as a forest. We will certainly examine Jesus' teachings, miracles, and familiar moments from his life. But we will also step back to understand the grand purpose of his mission, the larger story in which our individual stories belong.

The scope of the Gospel is vast. Its implications are far-reaching. Its power is immeasurable. Like forests, the Gospel is essential to human flourishing and, ultimately, to our survival.

Jesus entered the world with a mission unlike any before him. He saw people differently from his predecessors, his contemporaries, and those who would follow. He understood his role as prophet, priest, and king not only in a future age, but in the present one. Through his life and teaching, he introduced a worldview that affirmed the dignity and value of every person.

When Jesus healed the blind, the deaf, and the disabled; when he welcomed widows, orphans, and foreigners; when he confronted injustice and hypocrisy, he embodied the heart of Old Testament law. Love, mercy, and justice were not optional virtues. They were essential for humanity's well-being. Those who benefited from inequality and the preservation of the status quo found his message deeply threatening.

Part One of this study will focus on the Gospels of Matthew, Mark, and Luke, following the sequence of Jesus' ministry as presented by Matthew. But before we can understand the Kingdom of God that Jesus proclaimed, we must begin at the beginning—with Genesis.

Humans: Unique Creations

"In the beginning, God created the heavens and the earth" (Gen. 1:1). The earth was formless and empty, darkness covered the deep, and the Spirit of God hovered over the waters.

God brought order from chaos. He created light and darkness, sky and sea, land and vegetation, sun, moon, and stars. He filled the earth with living creatures. Then, at the climax of creation, God formed human beings. He breathed into them the breath of life, and they became living beings—free to live, love, learn, and grow.

Humans were unique among all God's creation. They alone were entrusted with responsibility for the world God had made. Twice in Genesis 1, God uses the word *rule*. The Hebrew term conveys stewardship, management, and dominion — not exploitation, but care.

"Let us make mankind in our image, after our likeness. And let them have dominion…" (Gen. 1:26–28).

Dominion was humanity's distinguishing gift. It was the capacity to steward creation wisely and to manage life in harmony with God's purposes.

Yet Adam and Eve faced the same temptation humanity has faced ever since: to place themselves at the center of the universe. The deceiver persuaded them that the garden existed for them alone, that they could define truth on their own terms, and that their choices carried no real consequences.

When they embraced that lie, shame and fear followed. Their relationship with God fractured. They became aware of good and evil but powerless to overcome its effects. By denying God's ownership of the garden, they lost their place within it.

Outside the garden, dominion vanished. Work became painful and unproductive. Relationships fractured. Hierarchy replaced equality. Childbirth brought pain. Sickness and death entered human experience. Violence soon followed, as Cain killed his brother Abel. Injustice, hatred, and suffering became woven into human history.

Humanity had lost its essential characteristic —dominion. No longer able to manage their own well-being, people suffered physically, spiritually, and socially. Even the natural environment bore the consequences of human irresponsibility. Inside the garden, humans exercised dominion over creation. Outside the garden, hunger, sickness, injustice, and fear exercised dominion over them.

Seventeenth-century philosopher Thomas Hobbes described life in its natural state as "solitary, poor, nasty, brutish, and short." His bleak assessment mirrors Adam's condition outside Eden—disempowered, impoverished, and hopeless.

It is a devastating thing to lose dominion over one's own life and story. History shows that when people lose the ability to define their own narrative, suffering follows. The horrors of the Holocaust would fade into abstraction if survivors did not insist on telling their story. The brutality of American slavery would be softened into myth if African Americans did not speak from lived experience. A battered spouse cannot allow an abuser to define reality. Adam and Eve lost dominion when they allowed another voice to tell their story.

God's Plan for Restoration

Humanity's failure did not end God's purpose. Another intervention was required, and God's plan for restoration unfolded through Moses and the Exodus.

At the burning bush, God revealed himself to Moses and declared his intent:

"I have seen the affliction of my people… I have heard their cry… I know their sufferings, and I have come down to deliver them" (Ex. 3:7–8).

Genesis, written by Moses from earlier sources and traditions, answered essential questions for a people enslaved for four hundred years: "Who are we? How did we get here? What caused us to lose dominion over our lives?"

Before liberation could occur, the people had to recover their story.

After the Exodus, Israel camped at Mount Sinai. David Brooks, in "The Second Mountain," describes the enslaved Israelites as fearful, passive, and unable to accept responsibility for their own lives—a people who had lost dominion. That condition is the essence of poverty: the loss of agency, dignity, and the ability to manage one's own well-being.

God's purpose, from creation onward, was abundant life—life marked by wholeness, justice, and peace. Slavery, inequality, and dehumanization were never part of that design.

Dominion Restored

God's promise to Israel was not merely freedom from Egypt, but restoration of purpose and agency—a return to dominion.

Bryant Myers, in "Walking with the Poor," reminds those engaged in ministry and communist development that God is already at work in communities long before you arrive. A Christian worldview recognizes God's ongoing presence, even amid brokenness. God sees. God hears. God knows. God acts. Trusting that truth is the beginning of restored dominion.

Disaster Response provides a contemporary example. Disasters—whether sudden or slow—strip communities of their ability to manage life. Effective response does not create dependency; it restores agency.

After Hurricane Irma flooded Good Samaritan Village in Florida in 2017, residents temporarily lost control over their lives. The goal of recovery was not merely cleanup, but the restoration of their ability to direct their own future.

A European Protestant denomination learned this lesson after the 2004 tsunami. Their evaluation concluded: "The success of disaster response is the community development that follows." In other words, true success is restored dominion.

The Kingdom of God

When John the Baptist and Jesus announced the arrival of the Kingdom of God, they proclaimed the restoration of dominion foretold by the prophet Isaiah:

"Of the increase of his government and peace there will be no end…" (Isa. 9:6–7).

Jesus concluded the Sermon on the Mount with a vivid image: lives built on obedience to his teaching would withstand storms; those built on anything else would collapse.

Jesus came to restore what was lost in Eden. He entered a world marked by economic, physical, emotional, and spiritual poverty—lost dominion. He proclaimed a better way.

When Jesus announced the Kingdom of God, he was saying: "You have lost dominion over your lives. I have come to restore it, so you may experience the fullness of life God intended from the beginning."

Discussion Questions

1. How does the concept of dominion in Genesis differ from how power is commonly understood today?
2. In what ways do you see "lost dominion" reflected in personal, social, or environmental brokenness?
3. What would restoring dominion look like in your own life or community?

Chapter 2: The Politics of Christmas

Luke 2:1-20

The first Christmas was not devoid of politics. The prophets who foretold the birth of the Messiah also spoke of a Prince of Peace, hinting at political implications of His reign. Isaiah prophesied that the government would rest on His shoulders. These are not mere religious musings but profound political themes. The Greek definition of politics is "relating to citizens, the process of making decisions applying to all members of each group."[1]

Historical context is significant to Jesus' birth narrative. It was a time when "God with us" was a new way for Him to relate to the citizens of the Earth.

> In those days, a decree went out from Caesar Augustus that all the world should be registered. This was the first registration when Quirinius was governor of Syria. And all went to be registered, each to his own town. And Joseph also went up from Galilee, from the town of Nazareth to Judea, to the city of David, which is called Bethlehem, because he was of the house and lineage of David, to be registered with Mary, his betrothed, who was with child. And while they were there, the time came for her to give birth. And she gave

---

[1] Henry George Liddell, Robert Scott, and Henry Stuart Jones, *A Greek–English Lexicon*, rev. and aug. (Oxford: Clarendon Press, 1940), s.v. **πολιτικός**, "of citizens, for citizens, or relating to citizens."

birth to her firstborn son and wrapped him in swaddling clothes and laid him in a manger, because there was no place for them in the inn. And in the same region, there were shepherds out in the field, keeping watch over their flock by night. And an angel of the Lord appeared to them, and the glory of the Lord shone around them, and they were filled with fear. And the angel said to them, "Fear not, for behold, I bring you good news of a great joy that will be for all the people. For unto you is born this day in the city of David a Savior, who is Christ the Lord. And this will be a sign for you: you will find a baby wrapped in swaddling clothes and lying in a manger. And suddenly there was with the angel a multitude of the heavenly host praising God and saying, "Glory to God in the highest, and on earth peace among those with whom he is pleased!" When the angels went away from them into heaven, the shepherds said to one another, "Let us go over to Bethlehem and see this thing that has happened, which the Lord has made known to us." And they went with haste and found Mary and Joseph, and the baby lying in a manger. And when they saw it, they made known the saying that had been told them concerning this child. And all who heard it wondered what the shepherds told them. But Mary treasured all these things, pondering them in her heart. And the shepherds returned, glorifying and praising God for all they had heard and seen, as it had been told them. And at the end of eight days, when he was circumcised, he was called Jesus, the name given by the angel before he was conceived in the womb (Lk. 2:1-21).

The Gospel of Luke records that Caesar Augustus issued a decree that all the world should be "apographo." In the New International Version (NIV), this word is translated as "census." The English

Standard Bible (ESV) refers to it as a "registration." The American Standard Version (ASV) says that the entire world should be "enrolled." The King James Version (KJV) says that all the world should be "taxed." Registrations and taxes are profoundly political. These were the circumstances surrounding the birth of Jesus.

The Registration

The 'registration' in the Christmas story is often seen merely as a logistical reason for Joseph and Mary's journey to Bethlehem. However, a closer look reveals that the word "registration" is mentioned four times in the first four verses of Luke 2, hinting at more profound implications that invite further exploration.

The Roman census was a strategic move in Rome's protracted and bitter struggle to assert dominance over Israel and the Jews, underscoring the political backdrop of the Christmas story.

Approximately four hundred years separate the last prophet of the Old Testament (Malachi) from the events of the New Testament. At the close of the Old Testament, Persia was the dominant superpower.

During the intertestamental period, Alexander the Great, and the Empire of Greece conquered Persia. When Alexander died at the youthful age of thirty-two, his empire was contentiously divided among four power blocks: the Ptolemy of Egypt; the Seleucids of Mesopotamia, Syria, and Central Asia; the Attalids of Anatolia (present-day Türkiye); and the Antigonids of Macedon (present-day Greece).

Palestine, that narrow strip of land at the east end of the Mediterranean, between the Sea and the deserts east of the Jordan River, was caught in the power struggle between the Ptolemys of Egypt to the south and the Seleucids of Syria to the north. In 63 BC, the Roman Republic conquered the entire region and attempted to establish Palestine as a client state. For the next 150 years, the Romans made repeated attempts through appointed Kings and Governors to bring the Jews to heel. In 37 A.D., Caesar appointed Herod I (The Great) as King of the region.

The death of Herod the Great in 4 BC created a power vacuum, and a struggle broke out among his offspring for political control of Palestine. During this time, a rebel named Judas of Gamala (not Judas the disciple of Jesus) led a zealot movement of Jews who resisted Rome, its census, and its taxes. Judas (the Galilean) said..."This taxation was no better than an introduction to slavery." The Zealot movement led to a series of violent wars, which culminated in the destruction of Jerusalem in 70 AD.

The registration, or census (mentioned in the first verses of Luke 2), increased resentment among the Jewish population and intensified the troubles. Shortly after Jesus 'birth, two Roman legions were sent from Syria to suppress the zealot rebellion, which was soundly defeated. Two thousand Jewish zealots were crucified, and about 6,000 young Galileans were deported as slaves to the western part of the empire. Jesus was born during this conflict. These circumstances clarify the reason that Joseph, Mary, and the young Jesus fled to Egypt for safety.

The Advent gives us insight into God's purpose. It introduces a New Kingdom, not a change in leadership or political philosophy, but a new way for humans to relate to one another and to God.

The Advent

In Latin, Advent means "coming, the arrival of a notable person, thing, or event." Words with similar meanings are appearance, emergence, materialization, surfacing, concurrence, dawn, origin, and birth. The advent of God in the world was an extraordinary event that changed the course of history, and its effects continue to influence us powerfully to this day. The Advent of Christ answers the question, "What would God do if He were to arrive on planet Earth?"

Peace Announced

The Advent story is about peace. "Peace on earth," the Angels sang. How can we miss that divine purpose? Peace is God's attitude towards us. Peace is God's gift to us.

The Gospel of the Kingdom is extraordinary; the ramifications of the Gospel are immense; the impact of the Gospel is enormous; and the power of the Gospel is vast. The promise of "Peace on Earth" is every person's hope, fulfilled!

How could the people of Jesus' time conceive of the possibility of peace? The Roman Army was crushing communities. Rome's forced registration uprooted people from their homes, disrupting the entire region. Taxation was random, harsh, and heavy. Infectious diseases were rampant; the average life span was thirty-two; orphans were ubiquitous. Unwanted babies were exposed or killed Slavery, including child slavery, was commonplace. Life was cheap. Furthermore, justice was often a matter of political expediency, taking the form of chains and crucifixion.

C.S. Lewis converted from atheism to Christianity because he could not account for the source of moral expectations. In his book, *Mere Christianity,* he asked why honesty and fairness are expected in business transactions. Why is robbery unacceptable? Why is murder universally a crime? Why is there a moral code that looks to protect weak and vulnerable humans when evolution teaches survival of the fittest? He found answers, not in the wisdom of human philosophy or science, but in the character of God, revealed in Jesus Christ, who introduced an unexpected way of life.[2]

One could ask the same question about peace. Who said people should live in peace? Who decided that peace is better than war and chaos? Why is peace a universally strived-for condition?

In the Gospel of the Kingdom, peace, proclaimed from Heaven, is an antidote for violence and brokenness. Peace is a robust concept that implies fulfillment, completion, maturity, soundness, wholeness, harmony, tranquility, security, well-being, welfare, friendship, agreement, success, and prosperity. Peace heals broken relationships between people and their Creator. Peace paves the way for a healthy, wholesome society.

The word "shalom" (translated as "peace") occurs more than 250 times in the Hebrew Bible and appears in 213 separate verses. In Classical Greek, peace is the state of law and order that gives rise to the blessing of prosperity. The word "peace" reflects peaceful conduct

---

[2] C. S. Lewis, *Mere Christianity* (New York: HarperOne, 1952), 13–16.

toward others and is found ninety-one times in the New Testament, with twenty-four of these instances occurring in the Gospels. Peace is God's intention for humans and is a central theme in the Bible, reflecting God's purpose in the Kingdom of God.

Peace is not private; it is interpersonal and communal in nature. Indeed, God did not announce "Peace on earth" to relegate it to individual hearts only.

God's Advent was not to change a leader or a political philosophy but to introduce an entirely new model for human relationships grounded in peace — peace with God and peace between people and "in" people.

David Brooks, an American author and political and cultural commentator, observes:

Our society suffers from a lack of connection and solidarity. We live in a culture of hyper-individualism. There is always a tension between self and society, between the individual and the group. Over the past sixty years, we have swung too far toward the self. The only way out is to rebalance, to build a culture that steers people toward relationships, community, and commitment — the things we most deeply yearn for are undermined by our hyper-individualistic way of life.[3]

---

[3] David Brooks, *The Second Mountain: The Quest for a Moral Life* (New York: Random House, 2019).

This hyper-individualism, Brooks calls mass narcissism. Narcissists are self-centered individuals who admire themselves and pursue self-gratification through vanity and sycophantic admiration of their idealized self. They have an insatiable need for affirmation and have an unconscious disinterest in anyone else's story or point of view. Trustworthy and honest conversation is not possible. Narcissists are not empathetic and will not admit wrong because they believe they can do no wrong. They explode with bursts of anger for no understandable reason and are exceedingly difficult to have a good relationship with.[4]

The shortcoming of social media is that it empowers hyper-individualistic narcissism. Individuals, separated by minutes or miles, explode with anger toward people they have never met. Furthermore, due to geographic distance, they do not experience the inconvenience of a face-to-face pushback.

However, with the Advent of Jesus, God comes near to live among dysfunctional people and points them to a better way. The peace that comes from God is both private and public, personal, and interpersonal, spiritual, and communal. Dominion is restored when people and communities experience God's peace.

---

4 . Mayo Clinic Staff, "Narcissistic Personality Disorder," *Mayo Clinic*, accessed March 14, 2026, https://www.mayoclinic.org/diseases-conditions/narcissistic-personality-disorder.

Opposing Power

The Advent of God challenged the underlying model of human relationships. Imagine if the Incarnation happened in the 21st century and the rebellion that opposed the Romans in Galilee were to happen now. An Army would be sent to confront the opposition with overwhelming force. That is what President Assad of Syria did in Homs in 1980 when the city's residents resisted his rule, and 80,000 people were gassed to death. Likewise, in Aleppo in 2016, the Russians bombed the city and killed civilians. It happened again in Mosul in 2017, when the Allies retook that city from ISIS. The Arab Spring in 2011 — a potential catalyst for peace — was thwarted by incumbent leaders. Humans are impressed by power and see it as a means to achieve peace.

For many (and perhaps most) political leaders, force is their first resort in resolving conflict. Force may win the day, but resentment, bitterness, and revolt will eventually erupt, spawning a new cycle of violence. Force may stop conflict, but it does not bring peace.

The same applies to personal disagreements. Too often, the natural human response is to use force. Yell louder. Use fists. Get a gun. In a climate of injustice, chaos, and fear, are we not often tempted, even encouraged, to react with force?

However, in an unfair, violent, oppressive political situation, God's efforts to establish peace did not begin with force of any kind. He did not confront power with a greater political or physical force. He sent a Savior as a baby, not a political leader.

The idea of the Savior implies deliverance through a superior plan and management of conflict rather than immediate victory over it. God, the all-powerful Creator of the universe, sent a baby into a world broiling with conflict and political oppression. What kind of threat is a newborn to a King? That "entrance" will never be considered a "power maneuver!"

The Christmas story teaches us that peace is God's valued gift to people. It shows we must remove force from the political and social equation to reach lasting peace. God's advent strategy, whether the conflict is with a spouse or the Internal Revenue Service, is to achieve peace. Stop the power plays and confront each volatile encounter or challenging situation with the same non-threatening approach as the Christ child's entrance on that first Christmas Day.

Unlikely People

God the Father chose an unlikely cast of characters to introduce His Kingdom: a pregnant, out-of-wedlock teenager, a righteous carpenter but reluctant fiancée, a helpless baby, adolescent shepherds, and Persian astrologers.

What is striking about the Advent story is how few "important" people take a leading part. Caesar has no part to play. The Syrian Governor is mentioned only as a time marker. King Herod is a minor character who hinders God's plan. The Chief Priest, the High Priests, the religious scholars — none are helpful in God's plan for peace and had little to do with restoring God's dominion.

The prophet Isaiah, looking forward to the coming Messiah, wrote centuries earlier: "Unto us, a child is born." Unto us: shepherds, carpenters, astrologers, priests, teachers, technicians, widows, farmers, financiers, plumbers, politicians, housewives, marketers, husbands, students, retirees, and working people — unto us a child is given, and the government (a new way of doing politics, a new set of beliefs and principals for life and relationships) shall be upon His shoulders. This new life of peace begins with His example, His way, made possible by His Spirit.

Christmas is the perfect time to ask ourselves: Is there a situation that needs peace? Is there a step that can be taken towards reconciliation, or a conflict that can be resolved? Deep and lasting joy is found by stepping out of the isolation of one's home, race, culture, and language and discovering friendship and fellowship across perceived barriers. Today, conflicts, big and small, are everywhere. Let us seek peace.

Many believers, expecting the Second Coming of Christ, say, "Come, Lord Jesus, come." That will be a momentous day! Nevertheless, the trumpet of Heaven announcing His arrival has not yet sounded. But Heaven's angels did announce: "Glory to God in the highest, Peace on earth."

Today, that same message echoes through time: A Savior is born. He is Christ the Lord.

For unlikely people like you and me, His coming has changed everything. We have peace with God, and the joy of pursuing peace with Creation and with one another. His Way leads to the renunciation of power, force, and violence, blossoming into caring, sharing, healing, and growing relationships.

Are we not all grateful that the Gospel of the Kingdom is a Gospel of Peace? Where would the world be without it?

Discussion Questions

1. Why does the author describe the Christmas story as inherently political?
2. How does Jesus' birth challenge conventional ideas of power and leadership?
3. Where are we tempted to seek peace through force rather than through God's way?

Chapter 3: The Kingdom Has Arrived

The New Testament opens with John the Baptist in the "wilderness of Judea" announcing the arrival of the Kingdom of God.[5] Adam and Eve, in Genesis 2:10-14, were expelled from the Garden of Eden and sent into the desert east of it.[6] Interestingly, Jesus began his ministry in the desert. There, while in prayer and fasting, preparing for His work of restoring dominion, Satan tempted him (Lk. 4; Mt. 4). The Evil One places a high value on denying dominion to God's creation, whether in a Garden or a desert. The Lord seeks out His people wherever they are.

Why did so many people follow John the Baptist? Was it because of his message? Luke 3:4-14 reads:

> And he (John) went into all the region around the Jordan, proclaiming a baptism of repentance for the forgiveness of sins. As it is written in the book of the words of Isaiah the prophet, "The voice of one crying in the wilderness: 'Prepare the way of the Lord, make his paths straight. Every valley shall be filled, and every mountain and hill shall be made low, and the crooked shall become straight, and the rough places shall become level ways, and all flesh

---

[5]Kingdom," in Strong's Exhaustive Concordance of the Bible.

[6] For geographical context, see "Mesopotamia," *Encyclopaedia Britannica*, accessed March 14, 2026, https://www.britannica.com/place/Mesopotamia-historical-region-Asia.

shall see the salvation of God.' He said, therefore, to the crowds that came out to be baptized by him, "You brood of vipers! Who warned you to flee from the wrath to come? Bear fruits in keeping with repentance. And do not begin to say to yourselves, 'We have Abraham as our father.' For I tell you, God is able from these stones to raise up children from Abraham. Even now the axe is laid to the root of the trees. Every tree therefore that does not bear good fruit is cut down and thrown into the fire." And the crowds asked him, "What shall we do?" And he answered them, "Whoever has two tunics is to share with him who has none, and whoever has food is to do likewise." Tax collectors also came to be baptized and said to him, "Teacher, what shall we do?" And he said to them, "Collect no more than you are authorized to do." Soldiers also asked him, "What shall we do?" And he said to them, "Do not extort money from anyone by threats or by false accusation and be content with your wages." As the people were in expectation, and all were questioning in their hearts concerning John whether he might be the Christ, John answered them all, saying, "I baptize you with water, but he who is mightier than I is coming, the strap of whose sandals I am not worthy to untie. He will baptize you with the Holy Spirit and with fire. His winnowing fork is in his hand, to clear his threshing floor and to gather the wheat into his barn, but the chaff he will burn with unquenchable fire (Lk. 3:3-17).

In first-century Israel, everyone expected the Messiah to come soon, and they were eager to know whether John the Baptist might be the promised One. John answered their questions, saying,

> I baptize you with water for repentance, but he who is coming after me is mightier than I, whose sandals I am not worthy to carry. He will baptize you with the Holy Spirit and with fire (Mt. 3:11).

John publicly criticized Herod Antipas, the ruler of Galilee, for marrying his brother's wife, Herodias. Consequently, Herod arrested John and imprisoned him. In his sermons, was John thinking about Herod when he addressed, "You brood of vipers?" What was he referring to when he said a tree was about to be cut down? What is the "fruit of repentance?"

The answer to these questions comes in response to three groups of people: the crowd, the tax collectors, and the soldiers who asked John, "What must we do?"

The Crowd

The Greek term "ochlos" (Lk. 3:10) refers to an unruly, large group of people. They were the first to ask, "What must we do?"

Ochlos is sometimes a Greek translation of the Hebrew word `am (people), or `am kābēd (a mighty people), when `am is paired with the Hebrew word erets (earth), connotes 'peasants of the land' *Erets* occurs 144 times in the Old Testament and calls attention to the social and religious status of peasants.[7] The Talmud applied the term to uneducated Jewish people.[8]

When John the Baptist announced that the kingdom of God had arrived, the 'people of the land 'were the center of his attention. Jewish peasants never had dominion over their lives, and John the Baptist and Jesus said that the Kingdom of God was for them.

The Gospel "for the poor" did not mean that their poverty somehow "saved them," but rather the poor were the center of God's attention. In that sense, the Gospel was theirs – it was <u>for</u> them. Blessed are the poor, Luke says, for theirs is the Kingdom of God.

In Walking with the Poor, Bryant Myers suggests that 'the poor are poor because others play the role of God in their lives.'[9] This was the plight of "the people of the land" in Jesus' time. The Roman government was so oppressive that the people had no agency over their own future. Excessive taxation kept people in a state of grinding poverty. The justice system punished them indiscriminately and cruelly,

---

[7]"Erets," *Bible Study Tools Hebrew Lexicon*, accessed March 14, 2026, https://www.biblestudytools.com/lexicons/hebrew/kjv/erets.html.

[8] Who Is an Am Ha'aretz?" *Yeshiva.org*, accessed March 14, 2026, https://www.yeshiva.org.

[9] Bryant L. Myers, Walking with the Poor: Principles and Practices of Transformational Development (Maryknoll, NY: Orbis Books, 1999), 73.

and the religious system burdened them with laws and rules. Others played the role of God in the lives of the poor.

The Kingdom of God arrived for them. The crowd liked the prospect of this new Kingdom and wanted to be a part of it — "What must we do?" they asked.

When we say that God is on the side of the poor, someone will respond, "But God also loves the "not poor!" Of course, he does! To say that the Kingdom of God focuses on the poor does not mean that it does not include the "better off" or the wealthy. Nevertheless, in God's Kingdom, there is no privileged first place. No special honor is assigned to wealth, position, class, education, or influence. All these typical advantages of wealth and power are not recognized in the Kingdom of God.

Jesus 'attention is not upon the wealthy and powerful, the usual center of society's attention, but upon the marginalized: the sick, disabled, women, children, and foreigners. He said *healthy people do not need a doctor, the sick do* (Mt. 9:12).

The Kingdom of God focuses upon the poor but requires that they produce the fruit of repentance: *if you have two coats, share one with someone who has none, and do the same with your food,* Jesus said.

This text is often interpreted to mean that those who are well off (have a surplus) should share their excess with those who are not. However, that is not the context of the peasants in John's time. Two coats did not make one wealthy. John was telling the "not so desperately poor" to give one of their coats and, if needed, some food to the desperately poor.

In the 1980s, Indonesian pastors from Borneo arrived on the island of Java with a small suitcase, ready to embark on their life in church ministry. They were carrying an extra shirt and pants, a second set of underwear, and a pair of good shoes. That is all they had to begin their life's work. It was like John asking them to give their second set of clothes to someone who had none.

To summarize, John is speaking to the impoverished, not to those with a surplus. He tells them that the fruit of repentance is that the not-so-desperate poor help the desperately poor.

John describes the Kingdom of God starting with the poor. Dominion is restored through compassion for the poor by people who have experienced poverty themselves – they no longer need to wait for justice, or alms, or temporary help from those in authority. Instead, they are called to minister to one another. This is the Kingdom of God at work.

Love practiced tangibly paves the way toward restored dominion. It frees a person from the stigma of poverty on the one hand and irresponsibility on the other. The Kingdom of God is for them.

CAMA Services (the Humanitarian arm of The Christian & Missionary Alliance) created a program in West Africa called Hands of Honor, started by Jane (not her real name), an American international worker.[10]According to the International Labor Organization, Northwest Africa has an extraordinarily high rate of child labor (59 million children are working, more than 21% of the region's children). In Mali, 56% of its children are engaged in child labor. In cities, affluent families hire domestic help, typically a young girl from a remote rural village. These girls, some as young as 11 years old, are hired to do home-bound domestic tasks for a decent wage, adequate food, and housing. However, their wages are often withheld for something as simple as chipping a plate or dulling a knife. They are verbally, physically, and often sexually abused. They have "lost their dominion." Influential people play the role of "God" in the lives of these children.

Jane developed "Hands of Honor" for these young girls, a program with a thoughtful and deliberate name. These girls think of themselves as "just hands" — hands to be used, directed, and owned, as if they were not attached to a body, soul, or family. The Hands of Honor program welcomes the girls into a dedicated, safe home.

Many girls outside this program become pregnant because of the abuse they experience in the homes where they work. When their pregnancy is discovered, they are expelled, with no place to go. Having been separated from their home, they have not seen mothering and are

---

[10]CAMA Services, "Hands of Honor," accessed March 14, 2026, https://www.camaservices.org.

unprepared to be mothers. Because of their humiliation, they resist returning home, even when a way is provided.

Hands of Honor provides a home for these girls. Jane loves, mentors, and trains them to prepare for motherhood and to care for others as they have been cared for.

One day, Jane overheard Botama, a longer-term resident, talking to a newcomer about the program. Botama said, "They will learn your name in this place — *they will know your name*!" A name, though not a tangible thing, is important! That someone who knew her name gave Botoma such dignity that she was eager to acknowledge someone else's name. Botoma became a believer and follower of Jesus Christ because of the compassion she was shown; she eagerly showered compassion upon other girls.

Love, expressed in something as simple as learning a poor girl's name, is the beginning of restoring dominion. This is what the Kingdom of God looks like.

The Tax Collectors

In Luke 3:12, the tax collectors asked John the Baptist, "What must we do?" John responded, "Do not collect any more than you must — be fair."

The tax collectors were not poor, but were powerful, and were despised in the New Testament world. The day they heard John the Baptist preach, surrounded by people whom they had extorted, they may have felt threatened and even envious that the Kingdom of God was offered to the poor. "What must WE do?" they asked John.

Their question betrayed an underlying concern: Was there a place in the Kingdom of God for them, the wealthy? Of course, there is! But like the poor, the rich were also to produce the fruit of repentance. For them, the fruit of repentance meant taking no more money from the people than the government required. This fruit of repentance is called "fairness."

Fairness restores dominion just as compassion does. The tax collectors had purchased the rights and authority to collect taxes from the local people on behalf of the Roman government. This gave them tremendous power, and they used it.

In the Roman world, the provinces carried the heavy burden of administering the Empire. Judea was part of the province of Syria, and every individual was required to pay 1% of their annual income as tax. There were also import and export taxes, crop taxes (1/10 of the grain crop, and one-fifth of wine, fruit, and olive oil), sales tax, property tax, emergency tax, etc. A Roman official, called a Censor, was responsible to Rome to collect the province's revenue. He auctioned the right to collect the tax to the highest bidders.

The tax collectors were from the local population. In this case, they were Jewish men who worked for the Roman Empire. As they collected the tax, they added a generous amount for themselves. Their reputations as petty tyrants and renegade extortioners were not conducive to their popularity. They knew their sin. Therefore, they asked John, "What must WE do?" John replied that they were *not* to collect more tax than was required.

Tax collectors took more than they should because they could; this explained why they bought the franchise in the first place. They wanted power over others to enrich themselves.

In 1979, after four years of language learning, cultural immersion, and community ministry, my family left Indonesia for a home leave. At the airport, as we exited the country, there were two emigration booths, each with an agent. No one else was waiting to be served. Our family of four stopped at the first booth, but the agent instructed us to go to the second booth. When we did, that agent told us to return to the first booth.

We realized that they were using our need for an exit stamp as leverage to extort a bribe. They used their authority or power to get "more than they were supposed to." With different methods but the same intentions, the New Testament tax collectors pressed those they "served" for more than they owed. John's answer to the tax collectors who asked, "What must we do?" applies to every worker, employer, employee, teacher, or government official, even to this day. Do not take more than is required! Be fair. In God's Kingdom, the fruit of repentance is fairness: not to take advantage of your position to extort more money (or anything) than is due.

In the West, some light-skinned people often oppress those with darker complexions because they believe culture allows it. Some men abuse women because they misinterpret Biblical or cultural practices as God-ordained. Some people bully others intensely because they believe it is their "human or Biblical right." Some who are wealthy extort the poor because they can. Aid workers in disaster zones sometimes do not listen to local people because they perceive themselves as experts.

Power differentials can be exploited as a means of extortion and manipulation.

In the Kingdom of God, fairness is a transformative force. The Kosovo CAMA ministry, "AGAPE," is working tirelessly to uphold this principle.[11]The Agape Center is making a difference in the lives of those with physical and mental disabilities who are without the financial means to pay for help. The community stigmatizes disabled people. Stigma refers to any aspect of an individual's identity that is devalued socially.

Susan (not her real name) is an international worker in Kosovo who cares for children with cerebral palsy. These children learn to use occupational therapy equipment, such as walkers and standers. Other clients have injured or arthritic hands and require hand splints. Susan provides physical therapy for these children, setting them on the path to becoming productive citizens. This happens in a Kosovo environment and culture, where caring for the physical needs of disabled poor children is considered impractical because disabled people appear "hopeless and useless" and are a financial burden to society. Therefore, care that could alleviate their affliction is rarely provided.

No wonder the Kingdom of God focuses upon fairness, because even disadvantaged, healthy people often stigmatize disabled members

---

[11] CAMA Services, "Health and Fitness for Kosovo," accessed March 14, 2026, https://www.camaservices.org.

in their long-established communities. This is NOT an acceptable practice in the Kingdom of God! Unlike the cultural practices around her, Susan, and her team care for poor and disabled people with fairness and loving concern. These children are recognized as God's creation and a central concern of God's attention.

C.S. Lewis wrote in *Mere Christianity:*

> Morality is concerned with three things. Firstly, with fair play and harmony between individuals. Secondly, with what might be called tidying up or harmonizing things inside everyone. Thirdly, with the general purpose of human life as a whole.... All people have always agreed (in theory) that human beings ought to be honest, kind, and helpful to one another.... A Christian society will not arrive until most of us want it.... But I cannot carry it out till I love my neighbor as myself, and I cannot learn to love my neighbor as myself until I learn to love God, and I cannot learn to love God except by learning to obey Him.[12]

When we act toward each other in fairness, not when we might choose, but as we ought, we produce the fruit of repentance. It is then that dominion is restored to us individually and to those with whom we interact. Lewis continued.

---

[12] C.□S. Lewis, *Mere Christianity* (New York: HarperOne, 1952), 69–72.

13. C.□S. Lewis, *Mere Christianity* (New York: HarperOne, 1952), 45–46.

> My argument against God was that the universe seemed cruel and unjust. But where did 'just' and 'unjust' come from? A man does not call a line crooked unless he has some idea of a straight line. What did I compare this universe with when I called it unjust? Justice means much more than the sort of thing that goes on in courts of law. Justice is about here (not over there or for somebody else), and it is personal and interpersonal.[13]

Acting and conducting business with fairness and treating people as equals in God's sight, no matter their status or physical development, are fundamental to life in the Kingdom of God. "Fair practice" is an essential characteristic that allows and promotes the restoration of dominion.

The Soldiers

The soldiers also asked John the Baptist, "What must we do?" John replied, "Be just."

Try to picture that day. In Luke chapter 3, John mentions "... crowds coming out to be baptized...." The crowds are "the poor," inspired by John's preaching that the Kingdom of God included them. John welcomed the peasants who had compassion for those who were worse off than themselves. He also opened a way for tax collectors to join the Kingdom of God, illustrating their change of heart through fair practices when collecting taxes for the government.

But what about the soldiers? Was there a place for them in the Kingdom of God? "What must we do?" they asked. John answered,

> Do not extort money from anyone through threats or false accusations and be content with your wages (Lk 3:14).

In Roman times, the purpose of the government apparatus was to serve the emperor. Power was delegated to government agents for the emperor's benefit. However, John changed all of that. In just a few statements, he said that government agents are responsible for doing justice for the poor. Do not extort, bribe, or falsely accuse them; protect the people.

Bryant Meyers describes the poor: "All their relationships are broken, unjust, and not for life."[14] Justice is fundamentally the way we treat each other. Restoring dominion is "doing justice."

I met a taxi driver in Ecuador traveling from Ambato to Quito. While traveling together in his car, he told his story: He had lived in New Jersey, USA, for nine years. To get there, he traveled through Colombia, Panama, Costa Rica, Nicaragua, Honduras, and Guatemala, through Mexico up to the US border. He hired a coyote (a person who guides immigrants across the desert) to lead him to the US border.

At the time, he said, the US had a special arrangement that allowed people from Costa Rica into the US. The coyote told him to tell the border agents that he was from Costa Rica, which he did. He crossed

---

[14] Myers, Walking with the Poor, 86.

the border and made his way to New Jersey. There, he found a job in a pharmaceutical factory. In a year or two, he married a woman (by common law) who was also an undocumented immigrant from Ecuador. They had a son. A brief time later, the police stopped him while he was driving on the New Jersey Turnpike. He was arrested and deported back to Ecuador.

When I met him in Ecuador in 2016, it had been five years since he had seen his son. He said that, under US law, he could not start the visa application process to re-enter the US until ten years had passed. Even then, he was unsure if he could obtain a tourist visa. His wife was afraid to leave the US for fear that she would be detained with no assurance that she could get back. If she took her son to Ecuador, it was also unclear if they could return to the US, even though their son was a US citizen.

The driver confessed that he should never have gone to the US. "I was wrong," he said. "Also, my wife should never have gone to the US. She was wrong. I should not have said I was from Costa Rica. That was wrong. But what are we to do now? We did what we did, and we have a son. We want to be together as a family, but we cannot. Like many others, we want to go to America, but our way is blocked."

As we chatted on that long ride from Ambato to Quito, Ecuador, my heart empathized with the driver. I identified with his longing for a job with a steady income to support his family, such as a construction or factory worker. I understood the unparalleled opportunity of raising a family in an environment where education and hard work ensured a return on his physical investment. I cried out for justice and mercy for this eager, loving father.

When we meet ordinary people face-to-face, hear their stories, and understand the walls of separation created only by the circumstances of birth, God's love for justice becomes clear. Often, justice has little to do with the law. Benjamin Franklin said, "Justice will not be served until those unaffected are as outraged as those who are."

If the taxi driver's story were my own, and I was kept from having a relationship with my son, I would be persistent, exploring every avenue at any price to be reunited. When we know and commune with someone, justice becomes a personal matter. Then, doing justice is the fruit of repentance, which restores dominion and brings the Kingdom of God into reality.

I am not advocating breaking the law, avoiding the law, or even changing the law. I am saying that when we meet and get to know people, matters of justice become both less complicated and more complicated at the same time. Better laws emerge when lawmakers begin from a place of compassion, fairness, and justice.

Restoring dominion — the Kingdom of God — is a transformative and profoundly impactful endeavor. We are called to travel the difficult road to restore peace, justice, and dominion, as God planned for each one of us.

John called the religious leaders a brood of vipers because they wanted to keep the old system of neglect, unfairness, and injustice for ordinary people. John said, "That system is coming to a fiery end."

The Kingdom of God had arrived. John described it as an environment characterized by compassion for the poor, power replaced by fairness in commerce, and governmental justice for the most vulnerable. The fruit of repentance is compassion, fairness, and justice, which flattens mountainous barriers of poverty, fills up the deep separating valleys of unfairness, and straightens the crooked ways of injustice.

Discussion Questions

1. What is the main idea or message of this chapter, and how does it challenge or confirm your current thinking?
2. Which example or concept in this chapter stood out most to you, and why?
3. How can the principles in this chapter be applied in a real-life situation (personally, in the church, or in the world)?

Chapter 4: The Kingdom Has Come

Matthew 6:9-13

In Matthew chapter 3, John the Baptist announced the arrival of the Kingdom of God. Jesus repeated that same announcement in Matthew 9:35.

The Jewish people anticipated a political Messiah who would deliver them from the heavy yoke of Roman rule. They expected that when the Messiah came, they would occupy positions of privilege and authority in the new Kingdom. Yet because of their preconceived ideas about what the Kingdom should look like, many failed to recognize it when it arrived.

Matthew shifts the reader's attention from John the Baptist to Jesus by recalling the prayer Jesus taught His disciples. This prayer reveals God's plan for His people, both in the present and in the future.

Our Father in heaven,
hallowed be your name.
Your kingdom come,
your will be done,
on earth as it is in heaven.
Give us this day our daily bread,
and forgive us our debts,
as we also have forgiven our debtors.
And lead us not into temptation but deliver us from evil.
(Matthew 6:9–13)

Jesus prayed that the earth would be like heaven—now. And He taught His followers to pray the same way.

When the Future Breaks into the Present

On my parents' farm, our family always looked forward to the harvest, which usually arrived around September 15. When that day came, the long wait for harvest time was over. Yet the harvest itself had only begun. For weeks afterward there was still work to do as the crops continued to be gathered.

In a similar way, Jesus prayed, *"Your Kingdom come."* The Kingdom has arrived, but it is still unfolding. The future has broken into the present, and the work of the Kingdom continues to grow and bear fruit.

This is what many theologians call the **"already—but not yet"** nature of the Kingdom of God. God's reign has begun through the ministry of Jesus, yet its full completion still lies ahead.

The New Testament Scholar N. T. Wright explains that when Jesus prayed for God's Kingdom to come, He was asking for God's rule to be established on earth as fully as it is in heaven. The prayer is not about escaping the earth for heaven; it is about God's restoring His rightful dominion over creation.

The apostle John the Apostle describes heaven in these words:

He will wipe away every tear from their eyes, and death shall be no more. Neither shall there be mourning, nor crying, nor pain anymore, for the former things have passed away. *(Revelation 21:4)*

Jesus prayed this way, and He taught us to pray the same prayer. Like Him, we can say:

"Lord, make this earth like heaven—a place where there are no tears of sorrow, no death, no pain, and no suffering."

That is what heaven is like, and Jesus wants the earth to reflect that reality.

Heaven is indeed the place where believers go when they die. Yet Jesus also calls His followers to live now in ways that reflect the values of heaven. Whenever God's will be done, whenever mercy triumphs over hatred, whenever justice replaces oppression, and whenever forgiveness overcomes bitterness, the Kingdom of God is breaking into the world.

An earth that increasingly resembles heaven is the kind of world Jesus teaches His followers to pray for—and to work toward—today.

In Matthew chapter three, John the Baptist announced the arrival of the Kingdom of God. Jesus repeated that announcement in Matthew 9:35.

Our Daily Needs

During the COVID-19 pandemic (2019-2022), we were not all healthcare workers heroically caring for the sick, or scientists laboring day and night to discover treatments and preventive vaccines, or philanthropists funding grand experiments to combat this pandemic. Despite our limitations, we could choose to isolate, wear masks, and take other recommended precautions to protect ourselves and others from infection. And we could pray: "Lord, make earth like Heaven now, eliminate this virus by whatever means, and restore your dominion over our lives."

Jesus prayed, "*Give us this day our daily bread.*" He prayed this way because he was (and is) concerned about physical life.

I was in Publix Supermarket on March 20, 2020, at the beginning of the quarantine related to the COVID-19 pandemic. No eggs were on the refrigerated shelves, and meat packages were scarce. All the cleaning supplies had been sold. The toilet paper was all gone. I thought to myself, could this virus affect our food supply in the United States? I was then reminded of people I met from around the world during my working years who struggled with daily food shortages, even before the COVID-19 pandemic. Here in the United States, I never worried about an inconsistent food supply, but Covid-19 raised that specter. It was a bold reminder that the Lord's prayer is essential to our everyday lives. "Give us, today, our daily bread. Please, Lord, meet our physical needs every day."

The Lord's prayer reminds us that we cannot have dominion over our well-being if our daily needs are unmet. Jesus knew that and taught us to express, through prayer, our daily reliance on God's gracious and good provision.

Forgive Us

Jesus also taught us to pray, *"forgive our sins as we forgive those who have sinned against us."* In this prayer, Jesus reminds us to regularly ask our Father to restore His dominion in our spiritual lives.

The Gift of Forgiveness, a book by Katherine Schwarzenegger Pratt, tells twenty-one stories of individuals who suffered profoundly at the hands of others and then made the deliberate decision to forgive. These are not ancient stories; they are stories of our time. Many of these tragedies unfolded in full view of the public and were widely reported in the news.

Elizabeth Smart was kidnapped at the age of fourteen and held captive for nine months, during which she was repeatedly abused. About a year after her rescue, she was asked whether she had forgiven her captors. She responded, "I felt like I had this epiphany of what true forgiveness was, and I remember feeling like, 'Yes, I have moved on. I have let it go. I have forgiven.'" Her insight was that forgiveness is an act of self-love. Holding on to a traumatic past does nothing but consume mental and emotional space.

Sarah Klein is one of the more than one hundred young female gymnasts abused by Olympic doctor Larry Nassar. She explained, "The more I forgive, the more I feel like I am not in an emotional prison anymore.… I must forgive to be free of him."

Scarlett Lewis, whose six-year-old son was killed in the Sandy Hook Elementary School massacre, said she wanted her surviving son, Jesse, to have a forgiving heart. She explained, "I want him to experience what I have grown to learn—that a forgiving heart is the only way to take back your power."

Immaculée Ilibagiza, a Rwandan woman, was a child in 1994 when she hid in a bathroom for ninety-one days while her neighbor systematically hunted down and murdered her family during the genocide. Years later, she intentionally met that neighbor while he was in prison. "This was a man I had known and respected like a father," she said, "and yet he was the one who had killed my family—all because our families belonged to different ethnic groups." She recalls breaking down in tears during their meeting, yet sensing that "even in my sadness, there was serenity and comfort deep down." She realized she did not want him to suffer. "It was then that I knew I had done the work to forgive him."

Polly Sheppard was the sole survivor of a prayer meeting at Emanuel African Methodist Episcopal Church in Charleston, South Carolina, when a gunman opened fire and killed nine members of her congregation. Polly came to believe that forgiving the shooter was essential to her healing. "I sit with all this unforgiveness," she said. "Who am I hurting? I am just hurting myself. I am holding on to sadness, frozen in grief." She later explained that she felt compassion for him, saying, "He is young and lost. He needs to accept Christ and repent for what he has done. If God forgives him, then he is forgiven."

Reflecting on her decision, Polly said, "You think you are letting someone off the hook, but when you forgive, you are letting yourself off the hook. If you do not forgive, you will not heal."

Desmond Tutu summarized the power of forgiveness this way: "When I talk of forgiveness, I mean the belief that you can come out the other side of a devastating experience and be a better person—better than one consumed by anger and hatred. Staying in that state locks you in victimhood and keeps you dependent on the perpetrator. If you can forgive, you are no longer chained to them. You can move on and even help them become a better person."

Most of us eventually come to this realization: if we are to be free from being consumed by those who have hurt us, we must forgive. This is what we ask the Lord to help us do when we pray—to release those who have sinned against us so that we ourselves may be free.

Another dimension of forgiveness is frequently overlooked.

Jesus' Forgiveness

When we recite the Lord's Prayer, we say, "forgive us our trespasses, as we also have forgiven those who trespass against us." This recognizes God's forgiveness, made possible through His sacrifice on the cross to mend our relationship with Him. By letting go of the wrong's others have done to us, we also release ourselves from the weight of seeking revenge, which some might call "just retribution."

Enduring the challenges of both giving and receiving forgiveness demonstrates restored authority and shows that God's Kingdom is present.

The last part of the Lord's Prayer asks for protection from evil: "Lead us not into temptation but deliver us from evil."

Jesus once asked, "How can someone enter a strong man's house and steal his possessions unless he first ties up the strong man?" He likened himself to the one who overcomes resistance, takes back what is rightfully his, and restores his rule.

Currently, the entire world faces quarantine. Over 7.6 billion people are staying home, away from work, schools, places of worship, entertainment venues, and restaurants. Many of us feel powerless, as if this virus has taken control over our lives.

During this time, George Floyd, a Black man, was killed by a white police officer. The officer pressed his knee on Floyd's neck for more than eight minutes. The policeman's nonchalant facial expression and relaxed body language, with his hand in his pocket, were captured on live video. People nearby were pleading for the police officer to let George up, while George can be heard begging for help repeatedly, saying, "I can't breathe."

One week later, another video showed a Black man being hunted down by off-duty police officers who shot the jogger in a suburb of Brunswick, Ga. Within the same period, in Louisville, Kentucky, police officers burst into the home of Breonna Taylor and shot and killed her in her bed while she slept.

The Bible directs us to "call out to the Lord, asking Him to deliver us from evil." Evil does not care that a man cannot breathe. It is Evil that hunts down a jogger and denies a young woman a safe sleep in her bed. These public sins must be called out for what they are — evil. Until we name them, we cannot be delivered from them.

Let us pray: "Lord, come, establish your dominion, your rule over the earth, now, please. We are afraid that we may lose the things that sustain our lives. Please give us what we need to live."

Let us pray: "Lord, forgive us, please, we humbly ask. Take away our sin and forgive us. Lord, help us to forgive others. Release us from the hurt others have caused us and help us let go of our unforgiving hearts towards them. Then Lord, we can live in harmony with our neighbors and enjoy Your dominion in our lives."

Let us pray, "Lord, keep us from evil. It lurks and beckons us with simplistic solutions to our real and imagined problems. We are tempted, Lord, by half-truths, lies, and false Messiahs. Lord, protect us from temptation and evil.

Father, we ask that You answer our prayer so we may know Your dominion in our lives."

Discussion Questions

1. What does John the Baptist mean by "the fruit of repentance," and how is it practical?
2. Why does the Kingdom of God focus so strongly on the poor and marginalized?
3. How do compassion, fairness, and justice restore dominion today?

Chapter 5: The Temptations

Matthew 4:1-11, Luke 4:14-22

In Matthew chapter 4, Satan attempts to tempt Jesus, and his proposals reveal what *he* believes Jesus' ministry ought to be. Luke chapter 4, by contrast, reveals the *actual* nature of Jesus' ministry.

Before Jesus begins his public work, John the Baptist clearly distinguishes his own role from that of the Messiah. In Luke 3:16 and Matthew 3:11, John declares, "I am not worthy to untie His sandals." In John 3:30 he adds, "He must increase; I must decrease." When he sees Jesus approaching, John announces, "Behold, the Lamb of God, who takes away the sin of the world" (John 1:29). He further explains, "I baptize you with water for repentance. But after me comes one who is more powerful than I… He will baptize you with the Holy Spirit and fire" (Matthew 3:11).

John understood that his message concerning the Kingdom of God was preparatory. He was a forerunner, not a ruler. His proclamation did not advocate political revolution or governmental reform. Rather, it pointed to a moral and spiritual kingdom marked by repentance, justice, compassion, and righteousness. While such values inevitably carry social implications, John anticipated a deeper and more comprehensive vision of the Kingdom—one that Jesus himself would fully articulate.

Following his encounter with John, Jesus is led into the wilderness. Mark records, "At once the Spirit sent Him into the desert, and He was in the desert forty days, tempted by Satan. He was with the wild animals, and angels attended Him" (Mark 1:12–13).

Both Matthew and Luke recount Jesus' temptation in the wilderness (Matthew 4:1–11; Luke 4:1–13). Their narratives are nearly identical, differing only in the sequence of the temptations. In each case, Satan tempts Jesus to define his mission in terms of **self-service**—through appetite, power, and wealth.

The Temptation of Appetite

Satan's first temptation appeals to physical hunger: "Tell these stones to become bread." Jesus responds in both Matthew and Luke, "Man does not live by bread alone, but by every word that comes from the mouth of God" (Matthew 4:4; Luke 4:4).

There is nothing inherently wrong with bread. Food sustains life, enabling our bodies to grow, think, adapt, and function. Yet Jesus exposes Satan's false premise—that human life is merely physical and can be fully satisfied by physical means.

Satan tempts Jesus to focus exclusively on meeting physical needs, as if that were the ultimate purpose of life. Jesus insists otherwise. Bread is necessary, but it is not sufficient. Life is sustained not only by food, but by God's Word.

This temptation persists today. Health, shelter, financial security, and material comfort are important, yet they easily become substitutes for meaning. Our institutions of higher learning and our media often define success in terms of money, power, possessions, or social approval. Yet a Gallup poll in January 2025 reported that Americans' average satisfaction across thirty-one areas of public life was only 38 percent—suggesting that material abundance has not produced contentment.

An empty soul seeks satisfaction through accumulation. Appetite, when unmoored from spiritual purpose, becomes a tyrant.

The Temptation of Power

The second temptation is the temptation of power. Satan takes Jesus to the pinnacle of the temple and says, "Throw yourself down."

Matthew describes how Satan places Jesus at the highest point of the holy city, tempting him to force God's hand and publicly demonstrate divine favor. This is not a call to trust God, but to manipulate Him—to gain influence through spectacle.

A vivid illustration of this temptation appears in the actions of the religious leaders themselves. The Pharisees initially opposed Roman rule, but when Jesus threatened their authority, they aligned with imperial power. They bribed Judas, negotiated with Herod, and ultimately warned Pilate, "If you let this man go, you are no friend of Caesar." In doing so, they bowed before the idol of power.

C.S. Lewis warned:

> Theocracy is the worst of all governments. If we must have a tyrant, a robber baron is far better than an inquisitor… The inquisitor, who mistakes his own cruelty and lust for power for the voice of Heaven, will torment us endlessly with the approval of his own conscience.

Henri Nouwen observed that many religious leaders succumb to the temptation of power for seemingly noble reasons:

> We tell ourselves that having power—if used for God or others—is good. History has repeatedly justified the Crusades, the Inquisition, slavery, the Holocaust, and countless genocides with this logic.

Nouwen concludes that power is often a substitute for love. It is easier to control people than to love them, easier to appear godlike than to obey God.

Jesus asks, "Do you love me?" Power tempts us instead to ask, "Can we sit at your right and left in your Kingdom?"

An observer outside the Church once remarked, "Evangelicals make no attempt to hide their pursuit of power because they equate winning with God's approval." God created us for something better than bowing to power.

The Temptation of Wealth

The third temptation is the temptation of wealth: "All this I will give you…"

Satan shows Jesus the kingdoms of the world and their splendor, offering them in exchange for worship. The offer is fraudulent. Satan owns nothing. He only traffics in what God has already created.

Jacques Ellul writes in *Money and Power*:

> Money has become the criterion for judging humanity and human activity. 'Being' has been made subordinate to 'having.'

This temptation is not merely about riches or authority. It is an invitation for Jesus to deny who He is—to abandon the truth that the world already belongs to Him as King of Kings and Lord of Lords.

Jesus responds decisively: "Away from me, Satan! For it is written: 'Worship the Lord your God and serve Him only.'"

We live surrounded by must-have things, illusory power, and relentless consumer desire. Ellul presses the question further: Are we truly alive, or do we merely exist? Our physical needs may be met, but is there a deeper dissatisfaction of the soul?

Even those who desire to serve God can become vulnerable—neglecting Scripture, following charismatic leaders uncritically, or adopting worldly values that quietly replace love with dominance and faith with force.

Let us not be satisfied merely with sustaining physical life. Let us live dependent on the gift of eternal life in Christ. Satan tempts our spirituality, our calling, and even our desire to serve. He invites us to sacrifice integrity for credibility, devotion for influence, and love for success. The result is always loss.

The Ministry of Jesus

Satan's temptations are invitations to serve the self. Jesus' ministry is an invitation to serve others.

Jesus defines his mission in Luke 4:18–19:

The Spirit of the Lord is upon me,
because he has anointed me
to preach good news to the poor.
He has sent me to proclaim freedom for the captives
and recovery of sight for the blind,

to set the oppressed free,
to proclaim the year of the Lord's favor.

Jesus' ministry is unmistakably other-centered. The poor, the imprisoned, the blind, and the oppressed stand at the center of his concern. Satan urges self-preservation. Jesus embodies self-giving love.

In the Kingdom of God, dominion is restored not by domination, but by love and service. Satan would have us destroy ourselves by serving ourselves. Jesus invites us to live by serving others.

The wilderness temptations expose two competing visions of life: one rooted in self-preservation, control, and possession; the other grounded in trust, service, and love. Satan offers shortcuts to influence and success, but Jesus reveals a kingdom shaped by faithfulness and compassion. The choice before every disciple is the same—whether we will define life by what we consume, command, or accumulate, or by whom we love and serve. In resisting temptation, Jesus does more than model obedience; He redefines power itself and invites us into a way of life that truly restores the world.

Discussion Questions

1. What does it mean to pray "Your kingdom come" in everyday life?
2. How does the "already but not yet" nature of the Kingdom shape Christian responsibility?
3. Where do forgiveness and daily dependence on God intersect in your life?

Chapter 6: The Sermon on The Mount

Matthew 5:1-16

In the Sermon on the Mount, Jesus contrasts the Kingdom of God with Judaism of his time. The Sermon has four parts: First, a prologue called the beatitudes, then a purpose statement, followed by two principal points, and a conclusion.

Prologue

There are nine beatitudes.

Blessed are the poor in Spirit, for theirs is the Kingdom of heaven.

Blessed are those who mourn, for they will be comforted.

Blessed are the meek, for they will inherit the earth.

Blessed are those who hunger and thirst for righteousness, for they will be filled.

Blessed are the merciful, for they will be shown mercy.

Blessed are the pure in heart, for they will see God.

Blessed are the peacemakers, for they will be called the children of God.

Blessed are those persecuted because of righteousness, for theirs is the kingdom of heaven.

Blessed are you when people insult you, persecute you, and falsely say all kinds of evil against you because of me. Rejoice and be glad because great is your reward in heaven, for, in the same way, the prophets before you were persecuted (Mt. 5:1-11).

People everywhere carry unseen burdens. Some may be grieving the loss of a loved one, or hoping for a merciful decision by a judge, or suffer in physical pain, or worry about the consequences of an unwise decision, or consider how to please an angry boss. Many people wonder where the next meal will come from. These are the burdens of the poor that rob them of dominion over their lives. When Jesus addressed the crowd in His Sermon on the Mount, he was not thinking of healthy people with wealth and security who lived confidently in comfort; he was addressing people who carried the mundane but heavy burdens of life.

Throughout the Gospels, the poor are the focus of Jesus 'attention. The Kingdom of God, he said, is for them. Luke's record of the first beatitude is unequivocal: *"Blessed are you, poor.*" Matthew's record is more nuanced: *"Blessed are the poor in Spirit."* In each account, the poor are blessed because the message of the Kingdom is directed at them.

That must have come as a shock to those who listened that day as Jesus preached. Few, if any, leaders valued the poor or made intentional efforts to address their situation. Few provided nothing more than alms or fashioned anything for their long-term benefit.

At that time, communicable diseases were rampant, and life expectancy was short. Fathers and mothers mourned the frequent early death of children. And children often mourned the death of their parents (the average life span was 32 years). The poor, estimated to be 80 to 90 percent of the population, longed for justice and relief from the cruel treatment by Rome. Jesus blessed the meek who suffered mistreatment from those who held positions of wealth and status in society.

Jesus blessed the peacemakers: the poor, who had the most to lose in conflict. He drew attention to their plight and raised their expectations for a better future.

The Beatitudes describe the situation of Jesus 'followers and offer insight into a better future: a new reality of comfort for the mourner, where the inner strengths of kindness and gentleness are valued, and justice, mercy, and peace are commonplace. In this new reality, God is found by the pure of heart, and peacemakers are called sons of God, and honor is given to those who stay true to Jesus in the face of fierce opposition. Jesus calls this "coming" and "already arrived" reality, the Kingdom of God.

Jesus did not impose a burden of shame and guilt on his listeners, nor did he require them to pay a price they could not afford or reach a goal they could not achieve. He called them "Blessed" as they were. "You," he says, "are the salt of the earth. You are the light of the world." The Beatitudes forever challenge the attitude of the powerful and wealthy toward ordinary people because God sees them as blessed. The Beatitudes call the rich and powerful to realign their worldview about the poor with God's view of them as His creation with purposeful futures. It is impossible to miss Jesus 'emphasis on "good deeds that glorify the Father," which are in stark contrast to the Jewish Priests 'rigid law-keeping.

After the prologue of the Beatitudes, we find the record of Jesus' powerful purpose statement:

> *You are the salt of the earth, but if salt has lost its taste, how shall its saltiness be restored? It is no longer good for anything except to be thrown out and trampled under people's feet. You are the light of the world. A city set on a hill cannot be hidden. Nor do people light a lamp and put it under a basket, but on a stand, and it gives light to all in the house. In the same way,* ***let your light shine before others, so that they may see your good works and give glory to your Father who is in heaven*** *(Mt. 5:13-16).*

Even today, some Christian teachings suggest that "good deeds" are optional. But good deeds create change, and Jesus said they glorify the Father in Heaven.

Exceed the Jewish Law

The Sermon on the Mount is set against the backdrop of the Second Temple interpretation of Jewish law, which was rigid and sought to preserve the status quo. Jesus instructed his followers to exceed the law. According to Matthew:

The law says:	Jesus says:
Do not murder: 5:21	Do not be angry.
Do not commit adultery: 5:27	Do not lust.
Do not divorce: 5:31	Do not be unfaithful.
Do not be a perjurer (do not lie) 5:33	Do not break any oath.
An eye for an eye: 5:38	Turn the other cheek.
Hate your enemies: 5:43	Love your enemies.
When you pray: 6:5-14	Do not be hypocrites.
Save money: 6:19-24	Store treasures in Heaven.

In His "Kingdom," people are less angry, less lustful, more faithful in marriage, truthful in their language, merciful in their judgments, generous in giving, loving (even) toward their enemies, private in their piety, and faithful to worship through prayer. They invest in eternal values rather than temporal things. This is an entirely new model for society and interpersonal relationships.

The Kingdom of God is a community of people following Jesus' example, not just to save themselves, but to join Him and others in His effort to reconcile the world to Himself. This does not mean everyone is called to be a pastor, preacher, missionary, or full-time Christian minister. It means that all of Jesus' followers, without exception, are committed to the things that Jesus is committed to — the Gospel of the Kingdom (restored dominion). These Kingdom principles may seem innocuous, weak, and ineffective. However, this is Christ's way, which pushes against the worldly, sinful structures that rob people of control over their lives.

Exchange with Private Piety

In the second half of the Sermon on the Mount (see Matthew, chapters 6 and 7), Jesus' second point is an exchange of public displays of religion (popular and expected then and now) for private piety.

- When you give, do so in secret (6:4).
- When you pray, go into your closet (6: 6).
- When you fast, do not "show off your fasting" (6:10).
- When you save your money, remember this: where your treasure is, there also is your heart (6:19).
- Do not judge others (7: 5).
- Avoid the wide road traveled by many (7:13).
- Enter the narrow gate with the few (7:13).

How do we live in this world while His Kingdom is coming into fruition? Jesus gives an extraordinary response! "*Do not worry! Seek the*

Kingdom of God and His righteousness (as listed above) and all these things will be added to you" (Mt. 6:23).

Jesus calls His followers to exceed the moral and religious norms of the day and exchange public religious hypocrisy for private piety! He adds, *"Then your Father, who sees what is done in secret, will reward you."*

Does Jesus expect these Kingdom values to guide our practices today?

Soon after arriving in Indonesia, Connie and I were assigned as "urban church planters" in Surabaya, East Java, the second-largest city in that nation. Although there were Christian churches in the city, none were associated with Gereja Kemah Injil (The Gospel Tabernacle Church), our Indonesian partner denomination. The Gospel Tabernacle Church in Surabaya was launched with two Javanese families and four college students — all young men. It was not too long before other families and students joined the group.

Their favorite worship chorus was: "Seek ye first the Kingdom of God and his righteousness and all these things will be added unto you…." We now understand what we did not understand then that those followers of Christ were known as Christians in their schools, workplaces, and neighborhoods. Moreover, because they were Christians, they were viewed as an apostate minority.

In those days, many radical Islamic political leaders and Presidential and Parliamentary candidates campaigned to make Indonesia an Islamic State. One campaign message was "death to the infidel." I heard that chant one day when I was caught in a huge political rally, surrounded by thousands of enthusiastic young people of the People's Islamic Political Party (PPP). That evening, our family heard that same loud slogan repeated from a rally at a mosque close to our house: "Death to the infidels."

Later, large trucks with open beds loaded with scores of young shouting demonstrators drove past our house repeatedly, chanting their slogans in unison. The Indonesian Christians also experienced these demonstrations. They felt threatened; more so than expatriates holding foreign passports.

When those youth of our church sang "Seek ye first the Kingdom of God…," they sang in hope and faith that God would give them all they needed, especially safety in an increasingly hostile community. They clung to Kingdom values: peace, kindness, truthfulness, generosity, meekness, and love for all people, including neighbors or friends who were followers of Islam. They believed that God would honor his promise of peace and protection. That was in 1978.

Did it matter that they tried to exceed the popular Islamic idea of righteousness? Did it matter that they exchanged popular public displays of religion with personal piety? What effect did their collective spiritual lives, together with other Christians in the country, have upon the structures of oppression that sought to keep them from God's gift of dominion?

When our family moved to fulfill a ministry call in the United States, I often returned to Indonesia for short visits. On one trip, a pastor friend told me that one of the candidates for Indonesia's Presidency had asked him to arrange a meeting with key Christian leaders. Indonesia was laboring to respond to Al-Qaeda-inspired terrorism in Southeast Asia. Al-Qaeda wanted to form an Islamic state stretching from Singapore, across Malaysia and Indonesia to the southern Philippines. To resist that movement, the Presidential candidate realized he needed the support of moderate Muslims and Christians. That was the first time that Christians had been consulted for political support. My friend joined with other believers to pray for and work with key government leaders, always conscious of obedience to God's Word.

About that same time, two of the largest religious organizations in Indonesia decided to distance themselves from other radical organizations in the Middle East and to seek peaceful relations with Indonesian Christian leaders. This illustrates God's mighty work in building and growing His Church in Indonesia. The Church of Jesus Christ, often viewed as weak due to its minority status, has not only been protected but has also experienced steady growth.[15]Today, Christ's faithful followers are prayer warriors and spiritual leaders in a culture that once sought to marginalize them or at least undermine their influence. They are a strong Church and share Jesus 'heart for a better world.

---

[15] On religious demographics in Indonesia, see U.S. Department of State, *International Religious Freedom Report*, accessed March 14, 2026, https://www.state.gov/religiousfreedomreport/.

Indonesian Christian leaders credit and praise God for these changes. However, they also remind us that, for decades, Christians have practiced the values of the Kingdom taught by Jesus in the Sermon on the Mount. As of 2018, Indonesia's 28.6 million Christians make up 10.72 percent of the country's population. The church in Indonesia is growing and is recognized as a faithful minority in an overwhelmingly Muslim country.

The way of Jesus may seem ineffective, but it is not! His way may be narrow, but it is the Kingdom Road. Jesus' way overturns sinful structures of oppression, providing hope for all, including the powerless and the poor.

Matthew 7:24-27 records Jesus 'conclusion of the Sermon on the Mount, mentioning "wisdom!"

> *Everyone then who hears these words of mine and does them will be like a wise man who built his house on the rock. The rain fell, the floods came, and the winds blew and beat on that house. It did not fall because its foundation was solid rock. And everyone who hears these words of mine and does not do them will be like a foolish man who built his house on the sand. And the rain fell, and the floods came, and the wind blew and beat against that house, and it fell, and great was the fall of it (Mt. 7:24-27).*

Those who do not listen to and do not practice Jesus' words will be like those who have built their houses on sand. When disaster arrives, the houses will collapse.

We are reminded of the "Temptations" recorded in Matthew chapter 3. A life dedicated solely to meeting physical needs, accumulating power, and pursuing wealth will not endure. Nevertheless, the people of the Kingdom of God who follow Jesus with whole hearts of faith and show their commitment with deeds of righteousness will survive Satan's fury. They will endure, have dominion over their lives, and be like a house built upon a rock.

Discussion Questions

1. How do the Beatitudes redefine who is considered "blessed"?
2. Why does Jesus insist that good deeds are essential rather than optional?
3. What does it look like to practice private piety in a public, performative culture?

Chapter 7: Watch Me

Matthew 8 and 9

The choice of stories and the arrangement of the events in Jesus ' life in the Gospels is interesting and informative. No Gospel writer records all or even most of the events of Jesus 'life.

For example, Matthew and Luke include Jesus 'birth narrative from different perspectives. Only Luke talks about the incident when Jesus was 12 years old and left behind at the Temple in Jerusalem after a visit there with his parents. These few events, recorded in the Gospels, are all we know about Jesus 'life from his birth until he began his ministry at the age of thirty.

Luke 1:1-4 says that "many have undertaken to draw up an account of the things fulfilled among us and handed down to eyewitnesses" and that he (Luke) carefully investigated "everything from the beginning" and "that it seemed good to him to write an orderly account." As an authoritative and scholarly historian, we can rely on Luke's account for a correct chronology of Jesus 'ministry.

Scholars have noted that all of Mark is included in Matthew and Luke and was a source for both writers. Mark's review was one of the eyewitnesses that Luke mentioned. There is also similar material in

Matthew and Luke that is not found in Mark.[16]Scholars surmise that Matthew and Luke consulted a common source, now lost.

There is also material in Matthew and Luke that is unique to each of them. That would be expected when several people write about the same event or person. We should be (and are) suspicious of exact duplicate accounts. A variety of perspectives and events unique to each writer, but with consistent characteristics, add to the Gospel's authenticity.

The Gospels are not biographies of Jesus—too much of His life is left out. However, there is fascinating agreement among the writers on which stories and events are included. This is evidence of the Holy Spirit guiding the writers to the events and teachings of Jesus that are essential for our understanding of the Kingdom of God. Scholars refer to this as the "stream of salvation history."[17]

The Gospel balances biography and pedagogy. Information about Jesus' life is balanced with details about what he taught. An overemphasis on Jesus' teaching could very well distract from His person. Too much emphasis on His day-to-day life might lead to

---

[16] For Markan Priority, see "Markan Priority," *Philosophy Dungeon*, accessed March 14, 2026, https://philosophydungeon.weebly.com.

[17] Martin J. Hoffman, "Prophecy and Fulfillment in the Old and New Testaments," *Journal of Biblical Studies* (1841–44).

idolizing His person at the expense of learning from His teaching. The Gospel is about Jesus AND his teaching.

The number of specific days of Jesus' life referenced in the Gospels is about forty. All the Gospel writers provide a consistent testimony, with nuanced details of the last week of His life. Of the other 33 days, all the writers carefully select events and teachings from life of over 30 years. These events and teachings illustrate and describe the Gospel of the Kingdom of God!

Matthew includes most of the stories and events of Jesus' life, which Luke also includes, but they are not presented sequentially according to Luke's chronology. This should not alarm us, as flashback and narrative rearrangement are employed in literature and film. This occurs in Matthew's account of Jesus' activities following the Sermon on the Mount. After He finished teaching and descended from the mountain (Mt. 8:1), the crowd, for the first time, saw the work of the Kingdom of God. The Sermon on the Mount was the classroom lecture, then Jesus went down the mountain into the laboratory of real life.

Paying attention to time indicators reveals that Chapters 5-11 span a few days.

Mt. 5:1: *When* he saw the crowd.

Mt. 8:1: *When* he came down from the mountain.

Mt. 8:5: *When* he entered Capernaum.

Mt. 8:14: *When* he came to Peter's house.

Mt. 8:18: *When* he saw the crowds around him.

Mt. 8:23: *Then* he got into a boat

Mt. 8:28: *When* he traversed the lake from one side to the other.

Mt. 9:18: *While* he was saying this.

Mt. 9:25: *After* the crowd had been put aside.

Mt. 9:27: *As he went* from there.

Mt. 9:32: *While* they were going out.

Mt. 9:35: Jesus *went* through all the towns and villages teaching, preaching, and healing.

Mt. 10:1: *He called* his disciples.

Mt. 11:1: *After Jesus finished* instructing his twelve disciples.

The words "then, while, after, he went on" indicate a continuous stream of events connected to and beginning with the Sermon on the Mount.

The Sermon addressed the poor; when he concluded His teaching, He came down from the mountain and met them. They included a person with leprosy who was shunned, isolated, and stigmatized; a Centurion who was hated as a feared foreign soldier; and a paralytic who had an illness that left him desperately poor and unable to move by himself. Matthew, the wealthy and disenchanted tax collector, was among those Jesus met. There was also a family with their friends attending a funeral for a young girl, and a poor woman with a bleeding ulcer. Matthew described some people as demon-possessed, while others were blind, mute, and lived a miserable, hopeless life.

The Old Testament instructed Jews to care for the vulnerable in their community.

> "'Cursed be anyone who moves his neighbor's landmark.' And all the people shall say, 'Amen.' 'Cursed be anyone who misleads a blind man on the road.' And all the people shall say, 'Amen.' 'Cursed be anyone who perverts the justice due to the sojourner, the fatherless, and the widow.' And all the people shall say, 'Amen'" (Deut. 27:17-19).

Isaiah said:

> Wash yourselves; make yourselves clean; remove the evil of your deeds from before my eyes; cease to do evil, learn to do good; seek justice, correct oppression; bring justice to the fatherless, plead the widow's cause. "Come now, let us reason together," says the Lord: though your sins are like scarlet, they shall be as white as snow; though they are red like crimson, they shall become like wool (Isa. 1:16-18).

Jesus lived out what the Old Testament taught, which was evidence that the Kingdom of God had arrived. His example and His teachings about the Kingdom changed how the world viewed people who suffer from that day forward.

Soon, Jesus would train and launch his disciples into the world to continue his ministry. Gary Frengren, in an article in Christian History entitled A New Era in Roman Healthcare, illuminates the situation they faced.

"Compassion was not a well-developed virtue among the pagan Romans. In the second century B.C., as in our day, many people began moving from the countryside to the city in search of jobs and amenities. Once in the cities, however, migrants found themselves living in tenement buildings, which lacked basic sanitary facilities. The support of family and village was lost; they eked out an often lonely, urban existence. They could expect no social support in daily alienation or trouble beyond occasional free grain and entertainment such as gladiatorial games ("bread and circuses").

Worse still, should they sicken, no clinics or hospitals existed to provide healing or basic nursing care. One could find physicians, but their fees were too steep for most. Some towns did hire a public physician, but institutional health care was unheard of. So, ordinary people were left to rely on healers and sellers of herbs, amulets, and quack remedies.

In a world of gods not renowned for their compassion, Roman culture did not encourage responsibility for assisting the destitute, the sick, or the dying. Individuals were expected to care for their health in any way they could. Many lacked even the safety net of family, such as discharged soldiers, peasants who had come into the city seeking work, or enslaved people who had been recently freed. Without a family, there was simply no support system: no one to care for you when sick, no one to help with food or rent when you could not work, no one to bury you when you died.

Destitute families, lacking resources to help, would sometimes abandon the chronically ill to die. In Rome, sick or elderly slaves were routinely left to waste on Tiber Island. Unwanted children were often left to die of exposure. If a father decided that the family could not afford to feed another child, that child would be abandoned on the steps of a temple or in the public square. Without exception, newborns with disabilities were exposed in a similar way.

Female infants were exposed much more often than males because a girl added another mouth to feed and could not (according to Roman social customs) work to support the family. Besides, the father knew he would eventually have to bear the burden of furnishing a dowry for each daughter's marriage.

Christians responded by demonstrating Christ's love to their brothers and sisters, who bore God's image (Jn. 13:34-35). The weaker and more helpless the neighbor, the greater the need to show them the compassion of Christ. Hence, early Christians showed special concern for the protection of unborn and newborn life. This practical morality departed radically from the social ethics of classical paganism, laying the foundation for Christian philanthropy.

The pagan idea of philanthropy (love of humanity) did not provide an impulse for private charity but actively discouraged it. In Greek and Roman society, beneficence (aiding the needy) existed primarily at the community level; civic philanthropy was exercised by rulers and the wealthy on behalf of the entire community,

> including both the rich and the poor. There was no reason to fund charitable institutions. The Stoic philosophy of many in the ruling class discouraged beneficence motivated by pity because it was based on emotion rather than on reason."[18]

Wholistic Christian ministry exemplified by Jesus continues today through Christian Relief and Development organizations committed to Christ-centered spiritual regeneration and human flourishing.

In 2006, an earthquake struck Central Java, Indonesia, with its epicenter in Klaten, approximately twenty kilometers from Yogyakarta. There, local churches partnered with World Relief to respond to the disaster. Church leaders collaborated with a local pastor to identify the most vulnerable people in the community. Then, with the church leaders, the pastor met with local village leaders to devise a response suitable for the community. They produced a brilliant idea: World Relief would provide resources to construct a "core room" in affected homes. That room was constructed to withstand a substantial earthquake. This included funding for a steel-reinforced 2x2 meter concrete foundation, six steel-reinforced concrete pillars, and a two-by-two-meter reinforced concrete ring at the top of those pillars. The villagers finished the walls with homemade bricks, which they did in record time. The safe room became a refuge from future quakes and a model for future homes in the village.

---

[18] Gary B. Ferngren, "A New Era in Roman Healthcare," *Christian History* (2011).

Due to the earthquake, farmers were compelled to prioritize their home repairs over cultivating their rice fields. The consequences of that would harm the future well-being of their families. For those farmers, the Indonesian partner (WRI) donated fertilizer for their crops, as the cost of repairing their homes had depleted their savings. For those without land, the national organization provided a pair of ducks. It is common to see "a poor person" leading a flock of ducks through the rice fields, allowing the ducks to eat the leftover or fallen grain. The duck owners could eat the duck eggs or sell or eat the offspring.

Because the pastor advocated for the poor and was faithful in visitation, he gained the trust of the whole community. Eventually, opportunities naturally opened, and the pastor presented the message of Christ to the entire village.

As a result, community leaders, guided by the national organization, identified the most vulnerable individuals in their community, provided practical assistance, and integrated disaster response into the church's ministry. Churches began to grow as they served the needs of the community. All agreed that Church-based disaster response should become a ready outreach ministry as climate change increasingly disrupts the status quo.

Migrants are the second area of modern vulnerability where the church can respond compassionately. This is not just an issue along the US southern border, but migration of oppressed people is happening across the globe. The primary causes of migration are clear: war, hunger, oppression, and a loss of economic opportunities.

Venezuela's 2020 economic crisis was an example of unexpected threats to life and well-being. The Venezuelan people were forced to flee to survive, not from the war, but from starvation. Food insecurity causes migration.

Inequity also causes migration. California has an economy larger than that of Great Britain. Florida's economy is equivalent to Indonesia's. New York's economy is similar in size to Canada's. Meanwhile, there are 120 million forcibly displaced people in the world, and 648 million people who live on less than $2.15/day. When a country's economy fails, people are forced into "survival mode," and they migrate to where there is an opportunity for their families to flourish.

Migration caused by despotism, breakdowns in civil society, and a loss of livelihood opportunities desperately needs a solution at the macro level. So, what can a local church do?

Indeed, we can pray and seek ways to engage church attendees in their community holistically. Churches can also form Indigenous partnerships with organizations that are making holistic, positive impact in vulnerable communities.

A church can also reevaluate its mission programs to determine whether its efforts restore dominion for the most vulnerable. Jesus modeled this when He came down from teaching the Sermon on the Mount to begin his outreach ministry among the poor, broken, suffering, and waiting communities.

Discussion Questions

1. Why does Matthew place Jesus' miracles immediately after the Sermon on the Mount?
2. What do Jesus' encounters reveal about God's priorities?
3. How can the Church today move from teaching into embodied action?

Chapter 8: Kingdom Training

Matthew 9:33 – 10:42

The biblical narrative in Matthew chapters 9 and 10 presents a vivid picture of Jesus caring for crowds who pressed toward him for healing. The people were astonished and said, *"Nothing like this has ever been seen in Israel."*

Jesus moved throughout towns and villages, teaching in synagogues, proclaiming the gospel of the Kingdom, and healing every disease and affliction. When he saw the crowds, he was filled with compassion, because they were harassed and helpless—*like sheep without a shepherd* (Mt. 9:35–36).

It was in this context that Jesus turned to his disciples and said, *"The harvest is plentiful, but the laborers are few. Therefore, pray earnestly to the Lord of the harvest to send out laborers into his harvest"* (Mt. 9:37–38).

What Was the Harvest?

Jesus was not speaking abstractly. The "harvest" was standing right in front of him.

It was:

- the stigmatized man with leprosy
- a hated Roman centurion and his servant
- undervalued women and girls
- a disgruntled but wealthy tax collector
- a desperate young man lowered through a roof.

- the blind, the mute, and the deaf

These were the people who occupied Jesus' heart. They were poor, vulnerable, overlooked, and—significantly—some were outside the Jewish faith. This was the harvest for which Jesus told his disciples to pray.

The Amplified Bible summarizes Jesus' instructions plainly: *"Heal the sick, raise the dead, cleanse the lepers, cast out demons. Freely you have received; freely give"* (Mt. 10:8).

This was no small assignment.

Healing, Then and Now

The disciples were encouraged to obey because they had just witnessed Jesus heal lepers, paralytics, a woman suffering from chronic illness, and people who were blind, deaf, and mute. He even raised a young girl from the dead.

Yet not everyone was healed. Not every sick person recovered. Not every dead child was raised.

That pattern has never changed.

Some were healed; many were not. Some experienced dramatic restoration, others continued to suffer. The Kingdom did not eliminate suffering—but it redefined it.

The stunning result of Jesus' healing ministry was not simply the number of miracles, but the way it transformed assumptions about illness and death. In the Roman world, sickness almost always led to death. The average lifespan was around thirty-two years. Illness and death were inseparable.

Jesus broke that fatalistic equation.

By healing some, he opened the possibility of life for many. He disrupted the inevitability of decline. The disciples were then sent to multiply this ministry—not merely by repeating miracles, but by stopping the cycle of sickness and death wherever possible.

That raises a crucial question:

How do we do this today?

Poverty in Pakis

Mrs. Jowo invited my wife, Connie, to visit Mrs. Suryo, who lived with her family in a tiny bamboo house with a dirt floor and a leaking roof. The room was so small that when the women sat facing each other, their knees touched.

Mrs. Suryo was pregnant, holding a baby while another child sat crying on the floor. An older boy stood in the corner arranging small cakes to sell at the market before school. Mr. Suryo was rarely home.

The crying child could not stand or walk and repeated only one phrase: "Mommy, I am hungry." Mrs. Suryo explained, "This child is already three years old, but she cannot walk."

That moment clarified the nature of the ministry needed. The family was spiritually open—but physically hungry.

Connie and Mrs. Jowo organized the women in our fellowship to provide one egg per day for protein and taught the family about locally available leafy greens. Within a month, the family began attending church—and the four-year-old was walking.

Eventually, Mr. Suryo came to faith and became one of three lay evangelists serving villages across East Java.

This was the fruit of repentance John the Baptist described: the poor showing compassion to those poorer still. It reflects exactly what Jesus sent his disciples to do—and what the early church practiced:

They shared possessions, broke bread together, and the Lord added daily those who were being saved (Acts 2:42–47).

Post-Disaster Nias Island

In March 2005, an earthquake devastated Nias Island, killing over a thousand people and destroying nearly every building. When I arrived a week later, the churches were strong—but something else was revealed.

Children were malnourished. Infant mortality was high. Typhus and dengue were widespread.

The most faithful response to Jesus' command to "heal the sick and raise the dead" was not dramatic miracles, but disease prevention.

World Relief implemented child survival programs: sanitation, clean water, mosquito control, and nutrition. When women resisted building latrines, a Bible study from Deuteronomy reframed sanitation as obedience to God. Within a year, disease rates fell dramatically.

Mothers regained the ability to manage their children's health. Dominion was restored.

Post-Genocide Cambodia

After the Cambodian genocide, World Relief introduced small community banks for women. Clinics followed. Then children's Bible and health lessons. Then house churches.

I once stood watching a puppet show for children while a nurse treated a dying woman under a nearby house. Men sat on porches listening from a distance. I remember thinking, *A church is being born here.*

These house churches became support groups for families with HIV/AIDS. I met couples who found Christ through these communities and discovered hope even in suffering.

Across post-war and post-disaster contexts, churches partnered with trained volunteers to deliver health education, monitor treatment, and care for the vulnerable.

This is what it means to heal the sick and raise the dead today.

The Restoration of Dominion

Beginning in the second century, Christians became known for nursing the sick. Hospitals, clinics, and medical schools emerged from this tradition. The impulse to heal did not replace faith, it flowed from it.

Jesus launched this movement by centering the poor and sending his disciples into the harvest.

This does not diminish miraculous healing, of which I am a grateful recipient. Rather, it affirms that Jesus cares for the whole person—body, soul, and community.

That is why he sent his disciples to proclaim that the Kingdom of God is near.

And that is still our task today.

Discussion Questions

1. Why does Jesus describe vulnerable people as the "harvest"?
2. How does healing today differ from—and resemble—healing in Jesus' ministry?
3. What does restoring dominion look like in disaster, poverty, or illness?

Chapter 9: Who is That Guy?

Matthew 11:1-19

"One Greater Than Is Here"

Matthew chapters 11 through 21 describe not only the extraordinary acts of Jesus but also the extraordinary claims he made about himself. His healings, his teaching—especially the Sermon on the Mount—and his growing popularity among the poor began to unsettle both civil and religious authorities. It was inevitable that questions about his authority would arise.

The leaders asked:

- Who is this man?
- Where did he come from?
- What is he really doing?

Jesus answered these questions—sometimes directly, sometimes implicitly—by making a series of startling claims. Five times in Matthew's Gospel he declared that something greater had arrived:

- greater than John the Baptist (Mt. 11:11)
- greater than the Temple (Mt. 12:6)
- greater than Solomon (Mt. 12:42)
- greater than the prophets (Mt. 12:18ff)
- greater than Satan (Mt. 12:22–28)

Each claim struck at the heart of Israel's religious, cultural, and political identity.

Greater Than John the Baptist

John the Baptist had announced the coming Kingdom with prophetic boldness. Yet when King Herod imprisoned him, John began to question whether Jesus truly was the Messiah he had proclaimed.

From prison, John heard reports of Jesus' ministry—healings, teachings, and miraculous works. He sent messengers with a direct question:

"Are you the One who is to come, or should we expect someone else?" (Mt. 11:3)

John's question revealed an expectation shared by many: that the Messiah would confront Roman oppression and inaugurate a political kingdom.

Jesus' answer defied those expectations:

"Go and tell John what you hear and see: the blind receive sight, the lame walk, lepers are cleansed, the deaf hear, the dead are raised, and good news is preached to the poor. Blessed is the one who is not offended by me." (Mt. 11:4–6)

John expected political upheaval. Jesus pointed instead to restored people.

The Kingdom had arrived—not through revolution, but through healing, mercy, and good news for the poor. This was a Kingdom concerned with human flourishing, not power.

Chronologically, John believed this Gospel **before** the crucifixion, the resurrection, the ascension, and Pentecost. He recognized the Messiah not through conquest, but through compassion.

Greater Than the Temple

Jesus' claim, "*One greater than the Temple is here*" (Mt. 12:6), was radical.

Judaism in Jesus' day was structured around Law, Land, and Temple. The Temple was the center of worship, sacrifice, and national identity. Yet Jesus repeatedly acted as though access to God no longer depended on it.

Later, he predicted that not one stone of the Temple would remain standing (Mt. 24:1–3). Within a generation, that prophecy was fulfilled. In 70 A.D., Roman forces destroyed Jerusalem and the Temple, ending the priestly sacrificial system.

Second Temple Judaism collapsed.

What replaced it was not another temple—but a people filled with the Holy Spirit.

At Pentecost, Jesus' followers were empowered and sent into the world. Sociologist Rodney Stark estimates that Christianity grew from a tiny minority in 100 A.D. to more than half of the Roman Empire by 350 A.D.

Indeed, Jesus proved to be greater than the Temple.

Greater Than Solomon

Solomon represented Israel's greatest political and economic success. Under his reign, the nation reached its widest influence and wealth.

Yet Solomon's kingdom fractured immediately after his death. What followed was decline, conquest, and exile.

Jesus declared that his Kingdom was greater—and history confirms it. Unlike Solomon's, Jesus' Kingdom did not diminish with time. It continues to expand across cultures and centuries.

His reign has no end.

Greater Than the Prophets

Jesus also claimed to surpass the prophets. He compared himself to Jonah, noting that while Jonah emerged alive after three days in the fish, he himself would rise from the grave after three days.

Jesus did not merely speak God's word—he embodied it.

He fulfilled Isaiah's vision of good news for the poor, freedom for captives, healing for the brokenhearted, and the year of the Lord's favor (Isa. 61:1–2).

As Eugene Cho observed during Holy Week, Jesus' journey to the Cross included confronting corruption, healing the sick, feeding the hungry, and washing feet.

The Kingdom of God is not merely about heaven—it is about justice.

Greater Than Satan

Jesus' authority extended beyond illness and institutions. He confronted Evil itself.

"If I drive out demons by the Spirit of God, then the Kingdom of God has come upon you" (Mt. 12:28).

Our culture often trivializes evil—through horror films, spectacle, or denial. Yet history repeatedly reveals its reality: genocide, mass violence, systemic injustice, and cruelty toward the vulnerable.

Evil flourishes when conscience is silenced and truth is distorted.

Jesus confronted Evil not only through exorcism, but through forgiveness, justice, compassion, and truth. In doing so, he restored dominion—the ability of people and communities to live as God intended.

Who Was Jesus?

The crowds loved him because he healed the sick. Women honored him because he valued them. Children trusted him because he welcomed them.

But religious and political leaders feared him.

When Jesus entered Jerusalem like a king, they understood the threat. If his movement continued, their way of life would collapse.

To preserve their power, they had to discredit the messenger.

Jesus knew this. He made his claims openly.

He was—and is—greater than John, the Temple, Solomon, the prophets, and Satan himself.

The Kingdom he proclaimed is neither political nor merely religious. It is a Kingdom of love, truth, justice, grace, and righteously by the King of Kings.

Living in his way remains the evidence that the Kingdom of God has come near.

Discussion Questions

1. Why were Jesus' claims so threatening to religious and political leaders?
2. What does it mean that Jesus is "greater than" the Temple, Solomon, and the prophets?
3. How does Jesus confront evil differently than the world expects?

Chapter 10: Ten Parables

Matthew 13:1-58; 20:1-16; 22:2-14

Matthew has twenty-eight parables about the Kingdom.[19]

Eight parables in chapter 13 begin with the phrase, "The Kingdom of Heaven is like..." These parables are about the Sower, the wheat and the tares, a mustard seed, yeast, a treasure hidden in a field, an expensive pearl, a net that catches all kinds of fish, a house filled with old and new treasures, and a wedding banquet.

Together, these parables teach us that the growth of the Kingdom of God is persistent while characterized as simultaneously tolerant, comprehensive, indispensable, heterogeneous, indifferent, and inflexible. Two parables illustrate each characteristic.

Because the Kingdom of God was unique, Jesus used many parables to explain it.

The Kingdom of God is Tolerant

"Simultaneous" means two or more events or conditions existing or occur at the same time, neither of which is dominant. For example, the 13th Amendment to the US Constitution, which gave freedom to slaves in the United States, became law on January 31, 1863. But the Civil War

---

[19]Matthew's "Kingdom of Heaven" corresponds to Luke's "Kingdom of God." See George Eldon Ladd, *A Theology of the New Testament* (Grand Rapids, MI: Eerdmans, 1974).

did not end until April 9, 1865. During the intervening two years and four months, were the African Americans, who were working without pay in the Southern Confederacy, enslaved or free? They were declared free, but still in bondage. Two conditions existed simultaneously.

In the parable of the Sower, the seed represented the message of the Kingdom of God. As the Sower spreads the seed, it falls on diverse soils. This is the key point of this parable. The farmer did not sow seeds on hard ground, then went to sow more seeds on rocky ground, then went to sow more among the thorns, and finally, sowed more seeds on good ground. Rather, as he sowed, the seeds fell everywhere on all kinds of soil. Some seeds could not grow, some seeds did not grow, some seeds were hindered after a good start, some seeds were choked by competition, and some seeds fell on good ground. Rejection and acceptance of the message of the Kingdom of God exists simultaneously.

Interestingly, some seeds fell on several types of fertile ground, producing yields of one hundredfold, sixtyfold, and thirtyfold. That is another simultaneous situation. The Lord says, "That is the way it is! Various levels of reception and implementation of the Kingdom of God's message exist simultaneously.

The parable of the weeds makes the simultaneous situation even clearer. A man sowed good seeds on his field, but then someone else planted weeds (tares) in the field while the owner was sleeping. The owner was dismayed when the plants sprouted, and he discovered wheat and tares in his field. His workers asked: "Should they pull up the weeds?" "No," the field owner explained, "the wheat and the tares must remain together until the harvest. If the bad are pulled up now, the good will be destroyed." The wheat must tolerate the tares until the harvest, pulling up the bad could ruin the good.

It does not alarm or bother the owner of the field that such a simultaneous situation exists. The principle is tolerance.

The Kingdom of God is Irrepressible

The Kingdom of God is irrepressible; this is the lesson of the parable of the mustard seed and yeast (Mt. 13:31-35). Mustard seeds and yeast are small and appear powerless, but they grow to have a profound impact on their environment, much like a pregnancy.

When we lived in a townhouse near Baltimore, our neighbors were a young couple who owned a sports car. They lived busy lives, coming and going at all times of the day and night. However, one day, they arrived home with a new SUV. I thought, "They must be planning on a family – maybe a baby is on the way!" Sure enough, a few months later, a new baby arrived. The small child had changed their lifestyle, including the type of car they would drive in the future. A few years later, Mike announced that they were building a new house. I thought, "They must be expecting another baby." Sure enough, a brief time later, a second baby caused them to seek a larger home because their current one was too small. Their lives were transformed and shaped by the arrival of children.

The Kingdom of God is like that. It takes root in our lives and alters how we perceive life, including what we own and how we live. It changes our futures, how we do business, and how we do our jobs. It affects our attitudes and activities, demeanor, goals, and ambitions — our entire way of life.

The Kingdom of God is irrepressible. It will change our outlooks, attitudes, plans, and visions, focus our hearts, capture our dreams, and shape our future.

The Kingdom of God is Indispensable

Matthew 13:44-46 includes two illustrations that help us understand the indispensable value of the Kingdom of God. The first story is about a man who found a hidden treasure in a field. He recognized its value, so he re-buried the treasure and then bought the whole field. Likewise, a merchant found a pearl. When he recognized its "great value," he sold all he owned to buy the pearl.

My life's work required international travel with multiple destinations. Finding homes and offices in foreign countries was a daunting task. However, Smartphones had recently come to market, and its GPS function easily led me to obscure addresses anywhere! It was indispensable for my work — I spent a considerable amount of money to buy one. The more I used it, the more I understood its handiness, and therefore, I could do more in less time. Besides a phone, it also had a Rolodex, an email system, a calendar, a to-do list, and a GPS! For most of us, smartphones have become an integral part of our daily lives.

The Kingdom of God is like that, but so much more. It is indispensable for life, providing guidance in relationships with people, conducting business, interacting with government, and nurturing families. The Kingdom of God is indispensable in restoring dominion in our lives.

The Kingdom of God is Heterogeneous

There are two parables about diversity (Mt.13:47-52): the first describes a net that catches a wide variety of fish, and the second is about a home that displays and protects both new and old treasures.

Diversity stimulates different perspectives for problem-solving and the development of social skills. The Kingdom of God is diverse. There are all kinds of people, from all levels of society with distinct cultures, languages, races, and social statuses, each with their unique contributions and views of life and the world. Excluding or hindering any one of God's children undermines restoring dominion to all God's people.

I met a South African lady who had lived in Namibia for many years. When I met her, she had recently moved to Zambia. She said, "I just love living abroad. It is refreshing, expanding one's vision of the world and the ways of doing things." She understood the richness and advantages of diversity. She reminded me that the Kingdom of God is diverse.

This aspect of the Kingdom of God is at risk in the early 21st century because nationalism is on the rise. Exclusivity is detrimental to growth, imagination, and exploration. In God's Kingdom, inclusiveness strengthens cooperation, growth, and innovation. We learn from each other. Restoration of dominion over our lives occurs when people work together to share experiences and knowledge, thereby leveraging growth.

The Kingdom of God, in sociological terms, is an open set that draws all people toward a central point, which is Christ. People in open sets are identified by whom they follow. Open sets are defined by openness, creativity, and growth. Closed sets are defined by requirements and restrictions that determine who is "in" and who is "out." Closed sets are defined by their borders.[20]

The Kingdom of God is an open set—Jesus said, "Follow me" (Mk 2:14), "Come and see, (Jn 1:46), "Come unto me, all ye that are weary and heavy laden, and I will give you rest" (Mt.11:28). The Kingdom of God is diverse because it is open to all people who will come and follow the Kingdom's leader.

The Kingdom of God is Indifferent

The Kingdom of God is indifferent to status, age, wealth, and influence (Mt. 20:1-16).

When we arrived in New England to begin our pastoral ministry there, a gentleman informed us that we were newcomers to the area, since his family had been there since the 1700s. I sometimes wish I had known then that my family had arrived in New England in the 1600s and had lived in the north ever since. (But it is probably better that I did not know that then. Even though I had the heritage, I still had much to learn!) A long, impressive pedigree or deep roots and social influence are meaningless in the Kingdom of God.

---

[20] Max Weber, *Economy and Society*, trans. Guenther Roth and Claus Wittich (Berkeley: University of California Press, 1978).

In the parable of the Vineyard Workers, "the all-day workers" thought they deserved more pay than workers hired "at the eleventh hour" (or late in the day). They were disappointed because they arrived first and thought they deserved more than those who showed up later.

However, that is not the calculus in the Kingdom of God. The thief on the cross, who was saved during the last minutes of his life, will have the same status in Heaven as the saints who gave a lifetime of service to their Lord. God's Kingdom is indifferent to the amount of time served following Jesus, or to social status, wealth, or influence.

The Kingdom of God is Inflexible

The parable of the banquet can be upsetting (Mt.22:1-14). It tells the story of a king who prepared a wedding banquet for his son, but the guests turned down his invitation. When the king realized the invited guests were not attending, he opened the banquet to everyone. Under the king's direction, servants entered the streets and gathered all the people they could find, good and bad. Thus, the wedding hall was filled with guests. However, when the king entered the banquet hall, he noticed one person who was not wearing wedding clothes. That man was "tied hand and foot and thrown outside." That action seems unfair! After all, everyone was invited. However, Mt. 22:14 warns, "many are invited, but few are chosen."

On the one hand, the Kingdom of God is open to everyone; all are invited. Nevertheless, there are conditions, illustrated in the above parable by proper dress, which is a metaphor of the requirement to enter the Kingdom of God. People "must dress themselves" with the confession that Jesus is Lord and follow Him. There are no exceptions! The Kingdom is inflexible.

Summary of the Parables

The Kingdom of God has arrived, but its propagation may be hindered by those who do not become rooted in its truth and sustained by its values. There will be opportunities to choose growth and development, but even those who accept the Kingdom's values may live them out imperfectly.

In the Lord's Kingdom, the good and the less good exist simultaneously. It is not our job to "pull up the tares." We must learn to be tolerant and leave judgment to God.

The Kingdom of God is also irrepressible. It will influence our growth and development, just as yeast changes bread dough, until Kingdom values shape every aspect of our lives. The Kingdom of God is indispensable for restoring dominion in all aspects of life. It is diverse, calling everyone into its dominion and grace. Moreover, it is inflexible, requiring repentance and following Jesus as Lord.

The Good News from Mathew is that the Kingdom of God has arrived. Although it is not a physical location or a governing body, it is a spiritual condition. More accurately, the Kingdom of God is a new way of life and is not confined by time. It is about a relationship with God, who is timeless, limitless, and boundless.

Just as important, the Kingdom of God is about relationships between people, NOT based on status, power, class, or wealth. Jesus said, "Come, all you who are weary and heavy laden, I will give you rest." There are no special qualifications to be met, except to believe in

Him. Jesus intends that the Kingdom of God become universal, but for the time being, it is tolerant, irrepressible, indispensable, diverse, indifferent, and inflexible.

Discussion Questions

1. Which characteristic of the Kingdom (tolerant, irrepressible, indispensable, etc.) stands out most to you?
2. Why does Jesus emphasize growth over immediate purity?
3. How do these parables challenge exclusivity or spiritual complacency?

Chapter 11: Restored Dominion and Judgment

Matthew 25

Jesus came to restore humanity's lost dominion.

Dominion was God's original gift to Adam and Eve—the ability to manage creation for their own well-being and for the flourishing of the world entrusted to them (Gen. 1:28–31). God provided abundant food for human beings and for every living creature. This state of well-being is captured in the Hebrew word **shalom**: peace, harmony, wholeness, completeness, prosperity, and welfare.

When humanity rejected God's design, shalom was lost.

Expulsion from the garden meant more than a change of location; it meant a loss of dominion. The ground was cursed. Work became toil. Pain increased. Competition replaced cooperation. Violence entered human relationships when Cain murdered Abel.

Inside the garden, humanity exercised dominion over creation. Outside the garden, creation exercised dominion over humanity.

This loss of dominion is the essence of poverty: the inability to manage one's own well-being. As Bryant Myers observed, all relationships become "broken, unjust, and not for life."

Where dominion is lost, shalom disappears.

The World Jesus Entered—and Ours

The world Jesus entered was marked by the same burdens we face today: preventable disease, hunger amid abundance, refugees fleeing violence, hardened hearts, injustice, corruption, greed, and exclusion. These conditions defined life under Roman rule.

They still define life in much of the world.

Yet Jesus proclaimed a way out—not through political revolution or religious performance, but through **entry into the Kingdom of God**, where dominion is restored and shalom begins to reappear.

Readiness for the Kingdom

Matthew chapters 23–25 record Jesus' final public teaching. Chapter 23 exposes hypocrisy. Chapter 24 warns of accountability. Chapter 25 presents three parables, each beginning with the same phrase:

"The Kingdom of Heaven is like…"

All three parables teach the same lesson: be ready.

The Ten Virgins

Readiness is not improvised at the last moment. Oil represents a life already shaped by Kingdom values. Those who lived prepared lives were welcomed. Those who ignored readiness found the door closed.

The Talents

What God entrusts to us is meant to be invested for his purposes. Readiness requires action. When the King returns, opportunity has ended.

These parables insist that Kingdom life is not passive belief, it is active participation.

Readiness Defined: Matthew 25:31–46

The final parable removes all ambiguity.

Readiness is defined by love expressed toward the vulnerable.

Jesus identifies himself with the hungry, thirsty, stranger, naked, sick, and imprisoned. To serve them is to serve him. To neglect them is to neglect him.

Judgment, Jesus says, will be based on how we treated "the least of these."

This is not symbolic language. It is concrete. It is physical. It is relational.

To spiritualize this parable is to empty it of its meaning.

Jesus places the highest priority on the essentials of life—food, water, clothing, shelter, care, and dignity—for **everyone**.

The Cost of Apathy

The sin of the "goats" is not cruelty—it is indifference.

Apathy allows hunger, sickness, and exclusion to persist. Apathy aligns with systems that prioritize profit over people, efficiency over dignity, and power over compassion.

I once spoke with a corporate executive in Zambia who reasoned that a woman on parental leave was a liability rather than an asset. He calculated loss to the company—but not cost to the woman, her family, or her community.

When profit eclipses compassion, dominion is stripped away.

The world's prevailing value systems often reward those who harm the vulnerable most efficiently.

The Sheep of His Pasture

The "sheep" are called blessed—not because they sought reward, but because love had reshaped them. They served without calculating worth, status, or return.

Throughout history, this love has taken institutional form: hospitals, schools, relief agencies, churches, and movements devoted to restoring dignity and independence.

Whenever the vulnerable are empowered and restored, dominion begins to reappear.

The Kingdom of God is made visible through these servant-leaders—now and forever.

Love as the Measure of Dominion

Near the end of his long life, the apostle John summarized eternal life in one word: **love**.

Jesus taught that love for God and love for neighbor are inseparable. Love confronts injustice. Love feeds the hungry. Love welcomes the stranger. Love threatens systems built on exploitation.

God's final judgment will be based on love lived out in concrete ways.

It is right to ask, *"What must we do?"*

John the Baptist answered that question simply:

- Be compassionate.
- Be fair.
- Be just.

We can do this. We can teach this. We can live this.

Dominion Restored

Before his ascension, Jesus said:

"All authority in heaven and on earth has been given to me. Go...

Jesus came to restore humanity's lost dominion. Dominion was God's gift to Adam and Eve, providing them with the ability to manage the Garden of Eden for their well-being and for the growth and development of the garden itself (Gen. 1: 28-31).

> God said, "every seed-bearing plant on the face of the whole earth and every tree that has fruit with seeds are yours for food." Plants also provided food for "all the beasts of the earth and all the birds of the air and all the creatures that move on the ground — everything that has the breath of life."

This "well-being" is defined as Shalom, a Hebrew word meaning peace, harmony, wholeness, completeness, prosperity, welfare, and tranquility.

The result of rejecting God's plan for humanity was expulsion from the garden and the loss of Shalom. The consequences for rejecting God's plan were grim. God said to Adam:

Cursed is the ground because of you (Adam); through painful toil, you will eat of it all the days of your life. It (the ground) will produce thorns and thistles, but you will eat the plants of the field.

Other consequences were that Eve's pain during childbirth would "greatly increase," and "the cursed ground resulted in painful toil." Another terrible consequence of the loss of Shalom was harmful competition between Adam and Eve's two children, resulting in the heartbreaking murder of Abel by his brother, Cain.

Although in the garden, Adam and Eve had dominion over all things, outside the garden, all things had dominion over them.

This is the essence of poverty; human beings have lost their ability to manage their well-being. All relationships, as Bryant Myers described, are "broken, unjust, and not for life."[21]

When millions of people die from preventable diseases, when the number of orphans multiplies because parents die too young, when thousands suffer hunger amid plenty, when war forces refugees to flee and host nations harden their hearts against them, when violence becomes commonplace, when money and power are the goals of life, when extreme individualism overtakes community, and poverty, injustice, greed, corruption, hatred, and discrimination flourish, dominion is lost as well as the evidence of Shalom. These were the burdens of the Israelites during the time of Jesus, when the Roman Empire ruled the world.

The people of earth struggle with these same burdens today. However, there is a solution, a way out of this poverty. Recognizing,

---

[21] Myers, Walking with the Poor, 86.

submitting to, entering, and participating in the Kingdom of God is the way to the restoration of peace and flourishing.

Matthew 23-25 records Jesus' last public ministry. Chapter 23 is a long warning against hypocrisy. In Chapter 24, as Jesus walked through the Temple in Jerusalem, he described the signs of the end of time, a time of accountability and the ultimate realization of Shalom. The last three parables in Chapter 25 are about readiness for and accountability at the judgment.

Like so many other segments in the book of Matthew, chapter 25 also begins with "the Kingdom of Heaven is like…." Here, Matthew recalls Jesus 'parable of the Ten Virgins. The kingdom of heaven will be like ten virgins who took their lamps and went out to meet the bridegroom. Five virgins were foolish, and five were wise. Five were ready for the groom because they had oil for their lamps. The five who were foolish fell asleep without checking their oil supply. At midnight, a cry woke the women: "Come out to meet the bridegroom!" The foolish virgins, without a supply of oil, were not ready for his arrival and were then shut out of the wedding feast. The thrust of the parable is to be ready for the groom's arrival, whenever that might happen.

The oil stands for the resources that the five virgins had gotten long before the groom arrived. They lived in readiness. Living a life dedicated to Kingdom values prepares one for the Lord's return. To ignore Kingdom values aligns us with those unprepared virgins who came late, found the door locked, and begged for entry, only to hear the bridegroom reply, "I tell you the truth, I do not know you." Matthew

25:13 states, "Therefore keep watch, because you do not know the day or the hour (when the bridegroom will arrive)."

The second parable in Matthew 25 is about ten bags of gold (better known as The Ten Talents). In this story, before he leaves on a long trip, the King distributes ten bags of gold among three of his servants. Two of the servants take the gold and earn more, but one servant takes his single bag and "saves it." That is, he does nothing with the gold.

The parable of the ten talents emphasizes the same lesson on readiness as told in the story of the ten virgins. Some servants take what they have been given, work with it, invest in it, and produce a significant increase. They are prepared when the King returns. They lived a life of work and readiness. However, one servant did nothing with the king's deposit. When the king returned, the opportunity for investment had passed and the servant had no return on investment for the king. Even if the two servants who were prepared for the king's return had wanted to help the slothful servant, it was too late!

These stories of gold and oil point to the values of the Kingdom of God. Some people devote their lives to loving and living for the things that the King loves. In contrast, others face the consequences of self-centered, destructive, and careless lives, showing no concern for creation, kingdom investments, or making the most of our God-given gifts and talents to serve His creation.

The final parable describes the coming of the Son of Man and judgment. Jesus says:

> *When the Son of Man comes in his glory, and all the angels with him, then he will sit on his glorious throne. Before him, all the nations will be gathered,*

and he will separate people from one another as a shepherd separates the sheep from the goats. Moreover, he will place the sheep on his right, but the goats on the left. Then the King will say to those on his right: 'Come, you who are blessed by my Father, inherit the kingdom prepared for you from the foundation of the world. For I was hungry, and you gave me food, I was thirsty, and you gave me a drink, I was a stranger, and you welcomed me, I was naked, and you clothed me, I was sick, and you visited me, I was in prison, and you came to me.' Then the righteous will answer him, saying, 'Lord, when did we see you hungry and feed you, or thirsty and give you drink? And when did we see you and welcome you, or naked and clothe you? Moreover, when did we see you sick or in prison and visit you?' And the King will answer them, 'Truly, I say to you, as you did it to one of the least of these my brothers, you did it to me.'

Then he will say to those on his left, 'Depart from me, you cursed, into the eternal fire prepared for the devil and his angels. For I was hungry, and you gave me no food, I was thirsty, and you gave me no drink, I was a stranger, and you did not welcome me, naked and you did not clothe me, sick and in prison, and you did not visit me.' Then they also will answer, saying, 'Lord, when did we see you hungry or thirsty or a stranger or naked or sick or in prison, and did not minister to you?' Then he will answer them, saying, 'Truly, I say to you, as you did not do it to one of the least of these, you did not do it to me.' Moreover, these will go away into eternal punishment, but the righteous into eternal life (Mt. 25:31-46).

The consistent theme of these three parables is to be ready. Judgment is coming; be ready. The parable of the coming of the Son of Man and judgment explains readiness. Jesus says that those who serve others, serve Him. Those who neglect the hungry, thirsty, or stranger, the naked, sick, or imprisoned, ALSO neglect their service to Him. God's judgment is based on how the vulnerable are cared for and served.

We began our study by reflecting on the message of John the Baptist. He challenged his listeners to produce the "fruit of repentance."

The crowd, the tax collectors, and the soldiers asked the same question: "What must we do?" John's answer was consistent. To the poor he said, "be compassionate to those who are poorer. To the merchant he said, "be fair in commerce." And to government agents he said, "be just."

Then, in the description of Satan's temptation of Jesus, we learned that satisfying our own physical needs and responding to the lure of wealth and power only continue patterns of oppression, which are opposite to Jesus 'commitment to restoration, recovery, release, and freedom for the oppressed, the sick, and the vulnerable.

In chapter five, Matthew records Jesus 'Sermon on the Mount. He describes the Kingdom of Heaven as radically different from contemporary religious practices. Then he demonstrated the practical implications of his Sermon by helping, healing, highlighting the needs of children and women, the sick, the neglected and the foreign-born. After that, he trained, empowered, and sent his disciples into communities to conduct ministries like his own: to welcome strangers, heal the sick, raise the dead, cleanse those with leprosy, and drive out evil spirits. And they did.

Twenty-eight parables in Matthew describe the Kingdom of God. We chose a few of those parables to describe the Kingdom and its implications for our contemporary setting. We noted that the Kingdom is synchronous, tolerant, irrepressible, indispensable, diverse, indifferent, and inflexible.

In the last parable of Matthew 25, we come full circle, back to Jesus's message to John the Baptist when he was in prison:

Moreover, Jesus answered them, "Go and tell John what you hear and see: the blind receive their sight and the lame walk, lepers are cleansed and the deaf hear, and the dead are raised up, and the poor have good news preached to them. And blessed is the one who is not offended by me" (Mt. 11:4-6).

In Matthew chapter 25, Jesus focuses on "the least of these" (verse 40). Final accountability, Jesus says, will be based upon how we treat "the least of these." They are the hungry, the thirsty, those needing clothes, the sick, the prisoner, and the stranger (or foreigners) who are in our community, at our workplace, schools, or places of worship.

Jesus shared this message only three or four days before the Passover, just before the crucifixion. It suggests that He thought about the vulnerable as he went to the cross.

The listeners who recognized themselves in Jesus 'reference to "goats" in the parable were shocked to learn that they had been judged negatively. They complained, "What did we do to deserve this?"

Jesus responded, "When I was hungry and thirsty, and a stranger, and needing clothes, and sick, and in prison, you did not help." Jesus so closely identified with the poor that not helping them was worthy of judgment. In Matthew 25:31, 41, Jesus says: "On judgement day, he will place the sheep on His right and the goats on the left. Then he will say to those on the left (the goats), "Depart from me…" The attitude of the "goats," as portrayed in Jesus 'story, was apathy at best and neglect at most.

This parable emphasizes the importance God places on human flourishing. Overlooking this point or spiritualizing it to redefine its plainly stated intent stunts the truth of the passage. Jesus places an extremely high priority on the essentials of life, including clean water, food, clothing, shelter, and protection – for everyone!

In this parable, the result of apathy is hunger, thirst, sickness, and imprisonment as experienced by "the stranger." We also learn that in the Kingdom of God, those who confess Jesus as Savior and Lord will confront forces that allow individuals, cultures, economies, or political systems to dismiss, overlook, turn away from, or ignore the spiritual and physical needs of the most vulnerable.

I met Michael (not his real name) in Zambia. He was the Director of a large multinational company and was trying to sort out a personnel issue that was causing financial losses to the company. He said, "If the company gives a woman a six-month pregnancy and parental leave, then we should conclude that we can get along without her work. She does not bring value to the company; she is more of a liability than an asset. I should consider replacing her with a machine, a one-time expense."

We understand the calculation of loss to the company. However, Michael did not calculate or take responsibility for the cost to the woman, her family, or her community.

The December 2018 issue of the UCLA Law Review features an article by Thomas Byrne. He states,

> "A brief historical survey reveals that although a corporation is a commercial enterprise, it was traditionally one that served the public good. Today, public good has been overtaken by the singular purpose to return value (wealth) to the stockholders."[22]

When the profit principle overtakes compassion for the most vulnerable, the consequences are devastating.

Recently, some donor countries have concluded that local corruption justifies a policy of "denying aid." Denying aid does not solve the problems faced by the most vulnerable in this and other similar countries. The world's prevailing value, focused on wealth accumulation, creates structures that undermine the welfare of the poor. It is alarming that the most educated, knowledgeable, powerful, and wealthiest individuals are too often those who neglect and inflict the most harm.

Throughout my life, it has been my privilege to have visited many countries, observing that the causes and symptoms of vulnerability are remarkably similar everywhere. Moreover, the wealthiest populations in each of these places aggressively seek and obtain solutions for

---

[22] Thomas Byrne, "False Profits: Reviving the Corporation's Public Purpose," *UCLA Law Review* (2010).

themselves, while too often ignoring the same pain and suffering in the lives of those around them.

It is difficult to understand that even among believers, suffering is judged as tolerable for some, but intolerable for others. As Jesus repeatedly reminded us, the most pressing problem to be solved is human selfishness.

In this parable, Jesus says that the sheep are "blessed." The listeners wonder why. Jesus said that it was because of their commitment to Him, as shown by their service to others without judging their status or position in society. Because of their authentic transformation, displayed through love for and service to others, they were ready for God's salvation and reward on the day of judgment.

Over the centuries, many organizations have been established to embody the love of Christ for the most vulnerable. The Salvation Army, YMCA, YWCA, World Vision, Mercy Corps, Tearfund, Cedar Fund, World Relief, Samaritan's Purse, Compassion International, and the Good Samaritan Society are just a few examples from a lengthy list of outstanding organizations doing "good work." These large and small ministries share the same vision: to display the love of Jesus Christ, in tangible ways, to the poor. Compassionate programs are also wrapped in the ministries of thousands of local churches. Moreover, secular and government agencies have taxpayer-funded "compassionate aid programs" that were born from or inspired by Christian values.

Each year, billions of dollars are willingly and enthusiastically given to support these causes. Nothing is more transformative or hopeful for both the generous giver and the implementing ministry than when hopeless and vulnerable people are empowered and restored to independent, productive living. The Kingdom of God comprises these selfless servant-leaders/followers, both in this life and next.

Many believers have dedicated their lives to carrying the message and practice of the Kingdom of God into remote villages, bustling cities, hostile quarters, or even into the competitive marketplace of ideas. You may be among these Jesus-followers. God bless you! You are one of Matthew 25's "sheep of his pasture."

The Apostle John followed Jesus for three years, listening to him teach about the Kingdom of God and seeing him in action. After 70 years of life (most spent in service to others), John reflected on Jesus' life and work. He summarized eternal life in one word: LOVE. Jesus said, "Love one another as I have loved you."

In Luke 10:2, we read, "Love the Lord your God with all your heart and with all your soul and with all your strength and with all your mind and love your neighbor as yourself."

The Kingdom of God is based on the ethic of love: love for all people! Love is displayed through compassion for the most vulnerable; love is fair and results in justice; love undermines all the ugly, hateful, manipulating, intimidating, cruel, dehumanizing, and satanic forces determined to deprive God's people of the dominion He planned and promised for us. The love of Christ, displayed by His sacrificial death on the Cross, threatens the sinful structures and petty justifications of religion that wrap people in rules and traditions, rather than leveraging the freedom provided by God's grace.

Christ's love also threatens governments that oppress rather than empower, or the greedy few who deprive dominion from the many, or Satan himself who "prowls around like a roaring lion looking for someone to devour" (1 Peter 5:8).

God's criteria for judgment will be based upon how we loved one another. This includes love for the vulnerable, the people who are so easily overlooked because they are hungry, thirsty, naked, sick, imprisoned, or are strangers in our midst. It is legitimate to ask after hearing Jesus 'message: "What must we do to demonstrate our love for the vulnerable?"

That is what John the Baptist was asked by the crowds that followed him when they first heard his message. John responded, "Be compassionate, be fair, be just." We can do that, advocate for that, and teach that message to our children and grandchildren. We can support these causes within our church, our communities, and our nation.

One more thing Jesus said:

All authority in heaven and on earth has been given to me. Go therefore and make disciples of all nations, baptizing them in the name of the Father and of the Son and the Holy Spirit, teaching them to observe all that I have commanded to you. Moreover, behold, I am with you always, to the end of the age" (Mt.28:18-20).

This is a massive task and a cosmic spiritual struggle. There is a colossal clash over who will hold dominion over the Kingdom of God, over who owns this universe, and whether there will be peace on earth.

Every day, let us pray earnestly: "Our Father in heaven, may Thy Kingdom come, thy will be done, on earth as it is in Heaven" (Mt. 6:10).

Discussion Questions

1. Why does Jesus make care for the vulnerable the measure of readiness?
2. How is apathy portrayed as spiritually dangerous?
3. Where might love require costly action rather than good?

Chapter 12: "Father, Forgive Them"

Luke 23:34

Jesus said,

Father, forgive them, for they do not know what they are doing" (Luke 23:34).

These are widely regarded as the first of Jesus' final sayings from the cross. No single Gospel records all seven, but the scholarly consensus is that forgiveness was the first word spoken in his agony.

Who did Jesus have in mind when he prayed this prayer?

There are at least four possibilities.

The Soldiers

First, Jesus surely had the Roman soldiers in mind—the men who nailed him to the cross.

Iron spikes were driven through his wrists and ankles. When the cross was raised and dropped into the ground, the sudden jolt tore further into bone and sinew. Crucifixion was designed not only to kill but to humiliate and terrify.

In the midst of that suffering, Jesus prayed,

"Father, forgive them."

Did the soldiers understand the depth of pain they inflicted? Perhaps not. Or perhaps empathy had been dulled by duty, repetition, and command.

Jesus taught,

"Do to others whatever you want them to do to you" (Matt. 7:12).

Yet here he embodied that teaching in the most public and costly way imaginable—by empathizing with the suffering of others through his own suffering.

Empathy at the Heart of Faith

Empathy is the capacity to understand and feel another person's experience from their perspective. It allows us to see through another's eyes and feel another's pain.

Psychologist Martin Hoffman argues that humans are born with the capacity for empathy. Christians recognize this as part of being created in God's image—because God himself is empathetic (Isa. 53:4).

Yet empathy does not always motivate action.

Brené Brown describes empathy as a skill grounded in perspective, taught or modeled in families. When one's worldview aligns tightly with a dominant culture, empathy for outsiders is often underdeveloped.

History reveals how leaders manipulate this weakness. When empathy for victims is suppressed and self-interest amplified, cruelty becomes possible. This was true in Nazi Germany—and likely true for Roman soldiers trained to execute without reflection.

Still, Jesus prayed,

"Father, forgive them."

Rome

Second, Jesus may have had the Roman government in mind.

Rome prided itself on law and order. Roman law shaped Western civilization. Yet this same system authorized the unjust execution of an innocent man.

They did not know what they were doing when they crucified Jesus under the banner of justice.

"Father, forgive them."

Religious Leaders

Third, the Jewish religious leaders stood nearby, approving the execution they had demanded (John 19).

They devoted themselves to the Law and the Prophets—yet violated the very ethic they taught. They urged Pilate to condemn a man they knew was innocent.

Jesus had summarized their Scriptures with a single command:

"Do to others as you would have them do to you."

Still, he prayed,

"Father, forgive them."

The Crowd

Finally, there was the crowd.

Like those who approved Stephen's execution in Acts, the crowd at Calvary watched and consented. Whether through fear, curiosity, moral confusion, or silent agreement, they participated.

Their failure was not direct violence—but apathy.

Jesus prayed,

"Father, forgive them."

Forgiveness and the End of the Cycle

Empathy and forgiveness must be learned—or re-ignited.

Not all families teach empathy. Not all cultures encourage it. Where empathy is stunted, indifference thrives.

We must look elsewhere for a consistent model.

We must look to Jesus.

Forgiveness is not denial, forgetting, or excusing harm. Psychologists define it as a conscious decision to release resentment and vengeance, regardless of whether the offender deserves it.

Forgiveness frees the wounded more than the offender.

Medical research confirms what Scripture has long taught: forgiveness reduces stress, lowers blood pressure, improves mental health, and restores relationships.

Unforgiveness traps us in the past. Forgiveness opens the future.

Grace on Display

On the day of the crucifixion, everyone involved worked in the presence of grace.

Jesus offered forgiveness before repentance was requested. That is grace—undeserved, unearned, freely given.

Pilate is remembered not for empathy, but for cowardice. The soldiers are nameless. Their apathy changed nothing.

But Jesus is remembered because his forgiveness changed everything.

He showed the off-ramp from endless cycles of resentment, retaliation, and violence.

Love that does not forgive is not love.

Resurrection Without Revenge

On the third day, Jesus rose.

Those who had condemned him expected retribution. Instead, they encountered forgiveness.

Jesus did not rise to punish his enemies. He rose to confirm his love—and to show a better way to live.

The Call to Imitation

Some say Christian values are dying. They point to cruelty, polarization, abuse, and cynicism as evidence.

Yet amid the noise, a quieter witness remains—followers of Christ who pray, even in loss and injustice, *"Father, forgive them."*

They are not naïve. They are courageous.

They understand that empathy and forgiveness are the only forces powerful enough to interrupt hatred and restore humanity.

Christ's followers are called to embody that way—showing empathy, grace, and forgiveness to all.

This is love that changes the world.

Discussion Questions

1. Who were the "them" Jesus prayed for, and why does that matter?
2. How are empathy and forgiveness connected?
3. What cycles of resentment could forgiveness interrupt in your life?

Chapter 13: I Will Be with You Always

Matthew 28:19-20

He Is With You: The Resurrection and Restored Presence

At dawn on Sunday morning, three days after Jesus was buried, a small group of women set out for the tomb. They carried spices, intending to anoint the dead body of Jesus, which had been placed hurriedly in Joseph of Arimathea's borrowed grave.

The Friday before had been agonizing. Jesus endured brutal physical torture on the cross. Mary, his mother, stood nearby and heard him cry out before giving up his spirit (Matt. 27:50). She watched Roman guards break the legs of the two criminals to hasten their deaths. Jesus' legs were spared, but a soldier pierced his side with a spear to confirm he was dead (John 19:32–33).

Pilate unexpectedly permitted Jesus' body to be removed and buried before sundown, prior to the Sabbath. A large stone was rolled across the tomb's entrance, sealed, and guarded to prevent tampering (Matt. 27:62–66).

The Empty Tomb

On the third day, the women approached the tomb, undoubtedly wondering how they could break the Roman seal and move the stone. Suddenly, the ground shook. An angel rolled the stone aside, and the guards collapsed in terror.

Matthew describes the angel's appearance as lightning. Mark speaks of a young man in a white robe. Luke recounts two men in gleaming garments who asked the women,

"Why do you look for the living among the dead? He is not here. He has risen."

When the women reported what they had seen, the disciples dismissed it as nonsense (Luke 24:11).

Mary Magdalene returned to the tomb and found it empty. She ran to tell Peter and John. They raced there, saw the grave clothes lying undisturbed, and returned home—confused, not convinced.

Mary lingered. She wept. She looked again. She encountered angels—and then Jesus himself. When he spoke her name,

"Mary,"

She recognized him.

She became the first witness of the resurrection.

From Doubt to Conviction

That same day, Jesus walked with two discouraged followers on the road to Emmaus. Later, he appeared to the disciples behind locked doors. Thomas doubted until he touched the scars.

Over the next forty days, Jesus appeared repeatedly—to individuals, to groups, to more than five hundred at once. He ate with them. He taught them. He reassured them.

These facts emerge clearly:

- The disciples doubted before they believed.
- The tomb was empty.
- Witnesses risked and gave their lives for this testimony.
- Jesus promised his continuing presence.

The Presence Released

Fifty days after Passover, on Pentecost, Jesus fulfilled that promise.

The Holy Spirit came with power. Languages were understood. Fear turned into courage. Peter declared that what the crowd was witnessing fulfilled the prophet, Joel.

Jesus was no longer merely *with* them—he was *in* them.

He Is Still With Us

That promise did not end in Jerusalem.

In 1978, in a crowded garage in Surabaya, East Java, a noisy motorcycle threatened to derail an Easter celebration. A simple prayer—"Lord, this is Easter; please stop the noise"—was answered immediately. The engine failed. Worship continued.

Months later, an unexpected missionary nurse appeared at our door precisely when our daughter needed medication—and disappeared just as quietly.

A theological student was warned away from danger by a stranger who vanished.

A grieving family in Indonesia found peace knowing that resurrection does not depend on burial location.

Decades later, that same truth resolved another family conflict—because confidence in Christ's dominion over death brings peace.

Presence as Restored Dominion

"The Lord bless you and keep you…

The Lord make his face shine upon you."

In Hebrew, face means presence.

When Adam and Eve were expelled from Eden, they lost God's presence. In Christ, that presence is restored. Restored dominion is not control over circumstances—it is **living consciously in the presence of God**.

Looking back, I now recognize that presence in childhood classrooms, college chapels, barns and tractors, hospital rooms, disaster zones, marriages, surgeries, grief, and joy.

Christian ministry is more than learning theology.

It is walking and working **with God present**.

That is the forest of grace in which individual lives find meaning.

That is peace.

That is restored dominion.

Part II

That You Might Live

Preface to John's Gospel

As a traveling Rabbi, the Apostle Paul's strategy of spreading the Good News was to visit and spend time in the synagogues found in the large cities of the Roman Empire. His purpose was to convince Jews that Jesus was the Messiah. In a brief time, however, he wore out his welcome. Upon leaving, he said, "Your blood be on your heads! I am innocent of it. From now on, I will go to the Gentiles" (Acts 18:6).

However, who were the Gentiles? The most common answer is that the Gentiles were not Jews, meaning they were Greeks. But who were the Greeks?

Today, the stories of the Old Testament and the history of the Jewish people are widely known through the creation story, the exodus of Israel from Egypt, the Ten Commandments, the Psalms of David, and the writings of the prophets. As the New Testament opens, John the Baptist and Jesus announce that the Kingdom of God had arrived. Matthew, Mark, and Luke record the ministry of Jesus to contemporary Jews, and thus we learn more about first-century Judaism.

Acts records Paul's missionary ministry, first to Hellenistic Jews of the diaspora, and then to the "Gentiles," i.e., Greeks. In his letters to new believers, Paul taught, corrected, disciplined, and continually distinguished the Way of Christ from Judaism. Thus, even in Paul's letters, we learn more about the Jews than we do the Greeks, who were choosing to become Christ followers in increasing numbers.

For contemporary readers of the Bible, the Greeks are relatively unknown, despite Western Christianity's rapid growth in its early Greek context. While the Gospel's Jewish context is obvious, its Greek context, in the early years of Christianity's spread, is also worth review. After all, America is influenced by Greek philosophy and culture as much as it is by Jewish history and religion.

Since John was the only surviving Apostle at the end of the first century, when the majority of believers (that is, followers of the teachings of Jesus) were Greek, my purpose in writing this brief study of John is to explore how John presented the Gospel to the Greeks and what attracted many Greek-speaking people to Jesus 'teachings. I will attempt to answer the question, "Who were the Greeks, and why, did the Gospel spread so rapidly among them?"

Chapter 14: A Cross-cultural Challenge

A Cross-Cultural Challenge

When the apostle John wrote his Gospel, he faced a challenge unlike that of the other Gospel writers.

Matthew, Mark, and Luke wrote primarily within a Jewish world. Their readers understood Israel's history, the Law of Moses, the prophets, and the long-standing hope for a coming Messiah. John, however, wrote from Ephesus to a Greek-speaking audience whose religious, philosophical, and cultural assumptions were fundamentally different.

For this reason, John's Gospel is not a summary of Jesus' ministry, nor is it a theological treatise like Romans, nor a pastoral letter like Paul's epistles. Instead, it is a carefully crafted cross-cultural presentation of Jesus, designed to lead Greek readers to one conclusion:

"These are written so that you may believe that Jesus is the Messiah, the Son of God, and that by believing you may have life in his name" (John 20:31).

The World John Addressed

The Greeks valued reason, democracy, philosophy, and civic participation. Thinkers such as Socrates, Plato, and Aristotle shaped how they understood truth, virtue, and the purpose of life. Greek religion, however, was mythological rather than moral. The gods demanded worship but offered little ethical guidance. Fate was inescapable. Death was final.

By contrast, Jewish faith was grounded in covenant, law, and history. Israel worshiped one God who acted in time, spoke through prophets, and demanded justice, mercy, and faithfulness.

John's challenge was clear: How could the Jewish Messiah be understood as God's Son by Greek minds without distorting the Gospel?

John's Strategy

John's answer was not argument, but encounter.

Rather than presenting abstract doctrine, John recounts six personal encounters Jesus had with individuals whose lives were disrupted, marginalized, or incomplete. These encounters are interwoven with six signs that reveal Jesus' identity and provoke belief.

John's Gospel unfolds as a series of lived experiences that invite the reader to ask:

What happens when ordinary people meet Jesus?

Each story moves someone from darkness to light, from confusion to clarity, from brokenness to life.

Belief and Life

Unlike the Synoptic Gospels, John rarely uses the word repent. Instead, he uses the word believe—more than eighty times.

For John's Greek readers, belief was not mere intellectual agreement. It implied trust, allegiance, and participation in a new way of life.

This is why John speaks repeatedly of eternal life—not simply as life after death, but as a present reality that begins when one believes.

Eternal life, in John's Gospel, is:

- relational
- transformative
- lived now
- completed later

It is the Greek-intelligible language for what the Synoptic Gospels call the Kingdom of God.

A Gospel for Greeks — and for Us

John's Gospel bridges cultures without compromise. He uses Greek language and concepts — truth, life, light, grace — and fills them with meaning rooted in Israel's Scriptures and fulfilled in Jesus.

The result is a Gospel that is authentically Christian and genuinely cross-cultural. The church in Ephesus did not become Jewish. It became Christian.

Preparing for What Follows

In the chapters that follow, we will walk with:

- a religious leader searching for meaning.
- a woman burdened by shame
- a man trapped in disability
- the accused and the forgotten
- the blind and the grieving

Each encounter reveals how belief in Jesus opens the door to life that begins now—life marked by freedom, dignity, healing, and hope.

This is the Kingdom you cannot see—but can experience.

Discussion Questions

1. Why did John write his Gospel differently from the Synoptic writers?
2. How does belief function as trust rather than mere agreement?
3. What barriers might prevent people today from encountering Jesus cross-culturally?

Chapter 15: The Greek Worldview

John's Purpose and the Shape of His Gospel

In John 20:31, the apostle states with remarkable clarity the purpose of his written account of Jesus' life, teachings, death, and resurrection:

"These things are written so that you may believe that Jesus is the Son of God, and that by believing you may have life in his name."

This single sentence governs everything John includes, and everything he deliberately omits. John did not write merely to preserve biography or supplement earlier accounts of Jesus' ministry. He wrote to form belief, and not belief as abstract assent, but belief that results in life. The verb believe, which appears eighty-five times in the Gospel, signals John's singular theological concern: belief in Jesus Christ as the Son of God is the means by which eternal life is received.

That purpose is reflected in the deliberate structure of the Gospel itself. John organizes his narrative into two clearly defined halves. Chapters 1–11 span approximately three years of Jesus' public ministry and center on a series of signs and personal encounters that progressively lead individuals to believe that Jesus is the Son of God. This first half reaches its climax in the death and resurrection of Lazarus. Chapters 12–21, by contrast, focus almost entirely on Jesus' final week—his suffering, death, resurrection, and post-resurrection appearances—and culminate in Jesus' own victory over death. Each half ends with death overcome by life. The very architecture of the Gospel proclaims John's message: belief leads to life.

Within the first half of the Gospel, John draws particular attention to six individuals whose lives intersect with Jesus in transformative ways. Each person follows a distinct path toward belief: a religious leader searching for certainty, a marginalized woman burdened by shame, a disabled man forgotten by society, a woman condemned by religious authorities, a blind beggar excluded from worship, and a grieving family confronted by the finality of death. Although these encounters took place more than sixty years before John wrote, their circumstances closely mirrored the lived realities of believers in Ephesus at the end of the first century. John's selection is neither accidental nor merely illustrative; these stories function as theological portraits through which belief and life are made visible.

Missional Challenge

John himself lived in Ephesus during the final decade of the first century, under the reign of the Roman emperor Domitian. Domitian's hostility toward Christians and Jews echoed the political fear and religious pressure that characterized the era of Jesus and the Herodian dynasty. Yet there was a significant difference between these two periods. By John's time, the Jewish Christian community was diminishing, while the number of Greek believers was steadily increasing. Many of these Gentile Christians possessed little familiarity with Israel's Scriptures or with Jewish Messianic expectations. The challenge John faced was therefore not simply one of preservation, but of communication. He was tasked with shepherding a fellowship that was fully Christian and genuinely Greek, communicating the Good News of Jesus faithfully and intelligibly within a cultural world shaped by different histories, philosophies, and assumptions.

This missional context helps explain why John writes so differently from Matthew, Mark, and Luke. The Synoptic Gospels recount Jesus' ministry largely through a Jewish framework, following a broadly chronological narrative shaped by Israel's story and expectations. John does something else. He omits the familiar birth narratives, the visit of the Magi, the shepherds and angels, Jesus' baptism and transfiguration, the exorcisms, the institution of the Lord's Supper, the Olivet Discourse, and Jesus' agony in Gethsemane. Instead, John records encounters—extended conversations and lived experiences in which belief is formed and life is transformed. His Gospel is not primarily chronological. It is pastoral and missional, shaped by theological intent rather than narrative completeness.

Nowhere is this clearer than in John's treatment of eternal life. In the Synoptic Gospels, the Kingdom of God is proclaimed primarily as a future hope rooted in Israel's Scriptures and often understood in political terms. Many Jews expected the Messiah to restore Israel's national prominence and establish God's reign visibly within history. In John's Gospel, eternal life becomes the central category. It functions as the Johannine equivalent of the Kingdom of God but expressed in language intelligible to a Greek audience. Eternal life is not merely future; it begins in the present. As Jesus declares, "I am the resurrection and the life. The one who believes in me will live, even though he dies." Eternal life, in John's theology, is the current experience of a future expectation.

This emphasis also explains John's striking preference for the language of belief over repentance. The term repentance does not appear in the Gospel at all. This absence is not theological oversight, nor does it signal a diminished moral vision. It reflects missional wisdom. For Greek readers unfamiliar with Israel's law and covenant history, repentance language carried little conceptual weight. Belief, by contrast, implied trust, allegiance, and participation in a new way of life. To believe was not simply to change one's mind, but to enter a new reality ordered around Jesus Christ.

Greek Philosophy

To accomplish this, John contextualizes the Gospel through philosophical categories familiar to Greek readers, not by neglecting them, but by re-forming them around Christ. Greek philosophy understood happiness (eudaimonia) as human flourishing achieved through reason and cultivated virtue. John redirects that pursuit, declaring that true life is found not through reason alone, but through belief in Jesus Christ as the Son of God. Truth (aletheia) was understood as unveiling reality, bringing what is hidden into the light. John proclaims that truth is no longer abstract or impersonal; it is revealed in the Word who was with God and was God. Reason (logos), long associated with rational discourse and meaning, is no longer an impersonal principle but has become flesh and dwelt among us. Life itself is reframed: bios, biological life that decays, is contrasted with zoe, life from God that endures. John writes so that his readers might receive zoe, life eternal. Even light, long associated with knowledge and enlightenment in Greek thought, is re-centered in Jesus Christ, the light that shines in the darkness and is not overcome.

Finally, John's treatment of grace (charis) resonates deeply within the Roman world of patronage. Grace was not sentiment but relationship—a dynamic exchange involving giving, receiving, and reciprocity. John presents Jesus as the embodiment of true grace: wine replenished at a wedding, dignity restored to the shamed, healing given to the forgotten, sight returned to the blind, and life restored to the dead. Those who receive grace are not passive recipients but participants in its movement, passing on to others what they themselves have received.

John illustrates this grace through ordinary lives: a bride and groom beginning their life together in joy, Nicodemus awakening to a Kingdom he could not see, a Samaritan woman becoming a witness to her community, a disabled man walking freely after years of dependence, a condemned woman released from shame, a blind man receiving sight, and Lazarus called from the grave. Each encounter reveals belief as entry into life, and each life becomes part of what may rightly be called the dance of grace.

Competing Worldviews: Darkness and Light

The Greeks inherited an elaborate and deeply tragic account of the origin of reality. As Cynthia Stokes Brown summarizes in her discussion of Greek cosmology, the beginning was not order or purpose, but Chaos—a yawning void from which emerged Gaia (the Earth) and a host of divine beings, including Eros, the Abyss, and Erebus, the shadowed realm associated with death. The Greek origin story is marked by violence, rivalry, and generational conflict among the gods themselves, culminating in Zeus's creation of Pandora, whose gift released suffering and evil into the world. The cosmos, on this account, is not the result of intentional goodness but of conflict, accident, and containment of chaos.

This origin story mattered. It shaped how Greeks understood life, suffering, power, and destiny. Reality was fundamentally unstable. Darkness was not something to be overcome so much as managed. Life was fragile, finite, and ultimately tragic.

John writes deliberately against this background. He does not merely offer new religious information; he offers an entirely different worldview. Where Greek cosmology began with Chaos, John begins with the Word. Where the Greek story explains life as bios—physical existence marked by decay and inevitability—John speaks of zoe, life that comes from God and is not overcome by death. One worldview moves inexorably toward darkness; the other announces light.

Modern scholars define a worldview as a constellation of beliefs, values, and expectations that shape how individuals interpret reality and guide their actions. A worldview answers fundamental questions: Who am I? What is the world like? What is wrong? For what can we hope? It determines how people assign value to themselves and others, how compassion and justice are extended or withheld, and how one faces the reality of death.

John does not deny darkness. He acknowledges it fully. "In him was life, and that life was the light of all humanity. The light shines in the darkness, and the darkness has not overcome it" (1:4–5). Darkness is real, but it is not ultimate.

This darkness takes different forms throughout the Gospel. Nicodemus, though a respected religious leader, lives in theological darkness, unable to perceive the Kingdom of God standing before him. The Samaritan woman exists in social darkness, isolated by ethnic hostility and personal shame. The man lying by the Pool of Bethesda embodies the darkness of despair—physically disabled, socially invisible, and resigned to neglect. In each case, darkness is not merely moral failure; it is a condition of existence shaped by distorted vision and diminished hope.

John exposes another form of darkness in chapter eight, where religious leaders attempt to trap Jesus by forcing him to choose between rigid legalism and mercy. Their confidence in their own righteousness blinds them to their participation in injustice. In chapter nine, that blindness becomes literal and symbolic: a man long ignored within the Temple is healed, only to be cast out by leaders more concerned with Sabbath regulations than with restored life. Their worldview cannot accommodate grace.

Even Jesus' closest followers are not immune. In chapter eleven, the disciples and Lazarus's sisters share a worldview in which death remains final. Their grief is honest, but their hope is limited. Jesus confronts that limitation directly, declaring, "I am the resurrection and the life." When Lazarus is raised, it is not merely a miracle; it is a revelation of a different way reality works.

On the evening before his death, Jesus gathers these threads into a single claim: "I am the way, the truth, and the life" (14:6). This is not a set of abstract propositions. Belief in Jesus is the entry point into a new way of seeing, a new understanding of truth, and a new experience of life. To believe is to adopt Jesus' worldview—to step out of darkness into light.

John writes with unwavering clarity about his purpose: "that you may believe that Jesus Christ is the Son of God, and that by believing you may have life in his name" (20:31). This life is not postponed until death. It begins now. It reorients how reality is understood, how people are valued, and how hope is sustained. John offers the Greeks of

Ephesus—and all who follow—a truer beginning, a brighter light, and a life that darkness cannot overcome.

Discussion Questions

1. How does John redefine life, truth, and belief for a Greek audience?
2. What competing worldviews shape how people understand meaning today?
3. How does belief in Jesus reframe success and fulfillment?

Chapter 16: About John and Ephesus

John, the son of Zebedee and brother of James, was among the first disciples called by Jesus from the fishing villages of northern Galilee. Together with Peter and Andrew, the sons of Zebedee left their nets at Jesus' invitation to "follow me," entering a three-year apprenticeship that would profoundly shape John's understanding of life, truth, and belief. John accompanied Jesus throughout his ministry, witnessing its defining moments. He was present in Jerusalem for the Passover, stood with Mary at the foot of the cross when Jesus was crucified, and was among the first to encounter the empty tomb. In the days that followed, John saw the risen Jesus in the Upper Room and during the forty days preceding the ascension.

After Jesus' ascension, John remained in Jerusalem with the other disciples until escalating persecution forced the early Christian community outward. The martyrdom of Stephen around A.D. 36, followed by Herod's execution of James, John's brother, marked a turning point. Leadership within the Jerusalem church was violently disrupted, and missionary attention shifted toward Judea, Samaria, and beyond. Political instability compounded religious pressure. Herod's death in A.D. 39, followed by upheaval in Rome and the eventual rise of Emperor Claudius, reshaped the Mediterranean world. Claudius' expulsion of Jews from Rome in A.D. 49 scattered Jewish and Jewish-Christian communities, sending figures such as Priscilla and Aquila eastward to Corinth and eventually Ephesus.

Although John's movements during these decades are not fully documented, early Christian testimony places him in Ephesus later in life, likely after the deaths of Peter and Paul and after the destruction of the Jerusalem Temple in A.D. 70. Irenaeus, citing Polycarp—himself a disciple of John—identifies John as the leading elder of the Ephesian church. By the time John arrived, Ephesus had become one of the most significant centers of Christian life in the eastern Roman Empire. According to Revelation 1:9, John was later exiled to the nearby island of Patmos during the reign of Emperor Domitian, whose persecution of Christians intensified during the final decades of the first century. These historical circumstances are essential for understanding the situation addressed by John's Gospel.

By the 90s A.D., the original apostolic leadership was gone. Jerusalem lay in ruins. Jews and Christians alike had been expelled from Rome. Christians were increasingly excluded from synagogues and regarded with suspicion by Roman authorities. The future of Christianity depended not on its survival in Jerusalem, but on whether the Gospel could be faithfully articulated in Greek and embodied within Greco-Roman urban life. Cities like Ephesus were decisive.

Ephesus

Ephesus was uniquely suited to shape the future of the Christian movement. Politically, it served as the administrative capital of the Roman province of Asia. Economically, it was a thriving port city, connected by major trade routes to Syria, Babylon, Egypt, and the wider Mediterranean world. Its prosperity, however, rested on fragile foundations. Over time, sediment from the Cayster River gradually filled the harbor, undermining the city's commercial lifeblood and foreshadowing its eventual abandonment. The rise and decline of Ephesus embodied the natural cycle of bios—birth, productivity, decay, and death.

Artemis

Religiously, Ephesus was dominated by the cult of Artemis. Her massive temple, one of the Seven Wonders of the Ancient World, drew pilgrims, tourists, and merchants from across the empire. Artemis represented fertility, protection, and prosperity, and devotion to her fueled a lucrative religious economy. Yet beneath the city's grandeur lay profound social darkness. Archaeological evidence points to widespread sexual exploitation, high infant mortality, and the routine disposal of unwanted children. The religious system that promised life and protection often delivered suffering and death.

The Library of Celsus

Ephesus was also a center of learning. The Library of Celsus housed thousands of scrolls, and the city was home to Heraclitus, whose philosophy of perpetual change shaped Greek reflection on reality. Reason, discourse, and the search for truth permeated Ephesian culture. When Paul preached there, he argued daily in the lecture hall of Tyrannus, engaging minds trained to value ideas. John would later address this same culture, but not primarily through abstract argument. He reasoned with the Ephesians by recounting lives transformed.

Slavery

Socially, Ephesus was built on slavery. By the end of the first century, tens of thousands of enslaved people lived in the city, branded, bought, and sold as property. Many of these enslaved men and women became followers of Jesus and were welcomed into the church as brothers and sisters. Paul's letters reflect this radical reordering of relationships, most notably in his appeal on behalf of Onesimus. That

Onesimus later became bishop of Ephesus stands as a powerful testimony to the Gospel's capacity to overturn entrenched hierarchies.

Women

Women likewise occupied a precarious position within Ephesian society. Denied legal equality, subjected to male authority, and surrounded by sexual exploitation, their lives were constrained by cultural norms that valued fertility over dignity. Against this backdrop, Christian teaching on marriage, mutual submission, and love took on countercultural force, offering women a status grounded not in utility but in shared life in Christ.

Jews

Ephesus also contained a substantial Jewish population, many of whom were Hellenistic Jews—Greek-speaking, culturally adapted, yet deeply committed to Israel's God. Paul began his ministry among them, reasoning from the Scriptures that Jesus was the Messiah. Some believed; many did not. Tensions between Jews and Christians persisted into John's lifetime, compounded by Roman suspicion toward both groups.

The Church

It was to this complex, fractured, and searching community that John wrote. The church in Ephesus was composed of former pagans and Jews, enslaved and free, men and women, educated and illiterate. They lived amid religious competition, economic uncertainty, political hostility, and social inequality. John wrote not to offer abstract doctrine, but to bear witness to Jesus through stories of belief and transformation. The six individuals he highlights in his Gospel are not random. They mirror the lives, fears, and hopes of the Ephesian believers themselves.

By recalling how ordinary people encountered Jesus and received life, John invited his readers into the same reality. Their experience of forgiveness, healing, and renewed allegiance marked the beginning of eternal life—not as distant hope, but as present participation. These stories have endured for millennia because they speak across cultures and centuries, bearing witness to a Gospel capable of re-forming lives, communities, and worldviews. John wrote for people like those in Ephesus—and for all who would hear his testimony and choose to believe.

Discussion Questions

1. How does John redefine life, truth, and belief for a Greek audience?
2. What competing worldviews shape how people understand meaning today?
3. How does belief in Jesus reframe success and fulfillment?

Chapter 17: The Kingdom You Cannot See

John 3:1-21

John does not tell the story of Jesus the way Matthew does. Matthew moves through proclamation and conflict in Israel's public life. John moves through **encounters**—carefully chosen moments when a single person meets Jesus and discovers that reality is not what they assumed it was. Earlier, John stated his purpose plainly: he writes "so that you may believe… and that by believing you may have life in his name." John 20:21.

John even shapes his Gospel around **six personal encounters**—individual lives in which belief becomes visible and eternal life begins now. He selects them because they mirror the lived world of his readers and because they expose life's deepest crises: the kind that imprison people from the inside and the outside.

Nicodemus is first—and he is first because his problem is the most dangerous.

Some problems are obviously tragic: sickness, disability, shame, death. Nicodemus' problem looks noble. It looks responsible. It looks like leadership. But it is spiritually compromised at the root: **the mixing of religion and politics.**

That mixture always promises life. And it always leads to death.

Believe

Jesus began his ministry at a wedding in Cana. The crisis was social and humiliating: the wine was about to run out. Jesus ordered the servants to fill six large stone jars—used for Jewish cleansing—with water. When the liquid was drawn out, it had become wine. Not merely wine, but the best of the feast. The master of ceremonies praised the host: "You have saved the best till last." □ cite□

John calls this a sign and records its effect: the disciples believed. □ cite□

The word *believe* runs through John's Gospel like a heartbeat. John uses it again and again—more than eighty times—and he uses it with intention. The Greek root (*pistis*) carries the meaning of faith, trust, and confidence—often used for loyalty and reliability, even in binding arrangements where something valuable is entrusted from one person to another. □ cite□

Belief does not merely agree with a statement. It is entrusting your life to a person. John is about to show what that costs—and what it gives.

Nicodemus

John introduces the first of the six encounters: the first is Nicodemus.

"Now there was a man of the Pharisees named Nicodemus, a ruler of the Jews. This man came to Jesus by night…" □ cite□

Nicodemus is not merely religious. He is **a religious professional** rabbinic scholar and a leader on the Sanhedrin council; a public teacher whose credibility depends on being seen as both faithful and wise. □ cite□

And he comes **at night**.

Night is not just a time marker in John. It is a spiritual and political atmosphere: secrecy, fear, risk, caution—the conditions that exist when speaking honestly can get you killed.

Nicodemus says:

"Rabbi, we know that you are a teacher come from God, for no one can do these signs that you do unless God is with him." □ cite□

Notice what he does not say.
He does not call Jesus Messiah.
He does not confess.
He tests the water.

Nicodemus is carrying a question that every leader under pressure carries:

What is safe to say aloud?

His world is filled with "rumors of war."

Rumors of War

John's Gospel assumes a background that modern readers can miss: the long, simmering conflict between Jewish messianic expectation and Roman imperial control. Many ordinary people hoped Jesus would be a conquering Messiah, and even the disciples carried political expectations and competed for positions of authority. □ cite□

Nicodemus is a leader in the middle of this.

If Rome suspected that a Sanhedrin leader was aligning with a messianic movement, the consequences could be catastrophic.

Nicodemus and Jesus could suffer the fate of other figures who inspired revolt. □ cite□

John traces the chain of tension:

Judas of Galilee and the resistance to registration and taxation—ending in brutal suppression, crucifixions, and exile. □ cite□

The persistent resentment that surfaces even in Gospel questions about taxes to Caesar. □ cite□

The choice of Barabbas—an insurrectionist—over Jesus at trial, revealing how deeply political hope had captured spiritual expectation. □ cite□

The rising pressure that continues after Jesus' ascension, including persecution and killings. □ cite□

And finally, the climax of the collision: Roman legions march; leaders die; Jerusalem is breached; inhabitants are massacred; the Temple is dismantled and its treasures carried off. □ cite□

This is where the mixing of religion and politics goes.

Not to renewal. To death. To the collapse of the world.

It is in that context—this looming inevitability—that Nicodemus comes at night wanting to "see the Kingdom."

And then Jesus says the most radical thing Nicodemus has ever heard.

The Kingdom You Cannot See

Jesus answers:

"No one can see the kingdom of God unless they are born again." □ cite□

Jesus' answer has two parts—and the first is often overlooked: **you cannot see the Kingdom.** □ cite□

Nicodemus wants a visible Kingdom—an identifiable political reality, a change of regime, a triumph of "our people," a sacred nation restored. Jesus interrupts him before he even finishes the thought.

Nicodemus is confused. How can an adult enter the womb and be born again? □ cite□

Jesus has to speak this way because Nicodemus' categories are too small. Nicodemus is trying to fit God's reign into the machinery of human dominance. But Jesus is describing something so different that it can only be received as **rebirth**—a whole new way of seeing.

To believe Jesus is the Son of God is to be introduced to a Kingdom you cannot see—**a spiritual reality with future fulfillment that begins now.**

This is why Nicodemus is the most religiously compromised. His problem is not that he lacks Scripture. His problem is that he has learned to survive—religiously and politically—inside a system where spiritual language is used to secure power.

Jesus does not merely challenge Nicodemus.
He attempts to save him—from the deathward trajectory of his world.

Scales Falling / Stepping Through the Wardrobe

Spiritual transformation is not the improvement of an existing worldview. It is the **collapse of one world** and the awakening into another.

Paul described his own transformation like blindness giving way to sight—like scales falling from his eyes. (And everyone who has been truly "converted" knows that feeling: the same facts remain, but reality rearranges.) When you are reborn, you do not merely add a belief. You receive a new perception, new moral gravity, new allegiance, new center.

C. S. Lewis captured the feel of it in *The Lion, the Witch, and the Wardrobe*: a child pushes through an ordinary-looking wardrobe and steps into another land. The air is different. The light is different. The rules are different. What seemed like a closed world suddenly is not. The deeper reality was there the whole time—but you could not enter it until you crossed a threshold.

That is what Jesus tells Nicodemus: **you must cross a threshold you cannot manufacture.**

Rebirth is not a political strategy.
It is the Spirit's miracle.

And it changes what you can see.

A Modern Parallel

This is not ancient only. It is present.

When Connie and I arrived in Indonesia for our first assignment in Surabaya, I went to the head of the Christian sub-sector of the Department of Religion to complete our local registration. We were required to present passports and process residency documents. □ cite□

Indonesia's context mattered. It was—and is—majority Muslim, and its government has long been vigilant against violent uprisings by radical movements seeking to impose a religious state. □ cite□

The official told me he had read the Indonesian Living Bible and believed it contained an error related to Matthew 10:4—where Simon is called a Zealot, with an added explanation about political struggle against Rome. □ cite□

Then he asked the question that revealed his fear:

Were we "Christian zealots"? Were we there to "see" a Kingdom in Java the way radicals wanted to "see" theirs—through political force? □ cite□

In that moment, Nicodemus was in the room again.

I reassured him: we had no political agenda. That is not what Jesus taught. Jesus was clear: **"You cannot see the Kingdom."** □ cite□

And the conversation turned. We came to an understanding: the Kingdom we proclaim is not an earthly theocracy. It is a spiritual reality entered through faith—transforming people, communities, and the way they relate to one another and to God. □ cite□

That distinction protected our work.
It also protected Indonesian believers—minority Christians whose safety can be endangered when Christianity is presented globally as a political takeover.

When Religion Becomes a Nation

In the United States, Christian nationalism has emerged as a budding movement eager to "see" a Kingdom—to make Christianity a state religion. □ cite□

Jesus' teaching stands in direct opposition to that impulse. A nation-state—no matter how religious—**is not the Kingdom of God**, and Christ's followers must resist the temptation to substitute political dominance for spiritual transformation. □ cite□

The stakes are not abstract. When Christians pursue power as proof of righteousness, they repeat Nicodemus' original mistake: trying to make the Kingdom visible by force, control, and identity politics. And history shows where that road leads: to enemies named as threats, to outsiders dehumanized, to fear baptized as virtue, to violence justified as necessary to death—social, spiritual, and sometimes literal death.

Jesus offers a different entrance: **rebirth.**

Waking Up in a New Country

Jesus says being born again is like waking up into a new world—and you captured that with lived precision.

Your first morning after landing in Jakarta, exhausted from a punishing journey, you were jolted awake by the 4 a.m. call to prayer—so loud it felt like the loudspeaker was in the room. Then thousands of mosques joined in, broadcasting prayer across a city of millions. □ cite□

We learned what it feels like to live inside a different worldview—where the rhythm of life revolves around prayer, where community matters more than individualism, where the pronoun "we" is valued over "I," where gestures and tone carry moral meaning, where loudness can be uncouth, where cultural "center" is assumed until you learn to see another center. □ cite□

That is the point: from infancy, people absorb an ethnocentric worldview as if it were universal. Being born again disrupts that. It is new life poured into the mind, heart, and soul—an awakening into a different country. □ cite□

Nicodemus thought he lived in the center of God's story. He still could not see the Kingdom standing in front of him because he expected a political Messiah. Jesus tells him: you will not perceive what I am doing until you are changed from the inside out.

The Kingdom Is Here

If this new worldview were fully lived, love of God and neighbor would replace fear and domination. Justice, mercy, humility, and hospitality would shape communal life. □ cite□

What the world would look like if people lived the commands Jesus repeated and embodied: love God and neighbor, do justice, love mercy, walk humbly, do to others what you would have done to you, care for the hungry and thirsty, welcome the stranger. □ cite□

If that occurred within cultures and languages and nations—without coercion—then it could be said that Jesus was King spiritually, personally, and communally, and that the Kingdom had arrived. □ cite□

Not as a regime. As life.

The Kingdom would not be seen politically, but as a realized truth—a way of life caused by spiritual transformation. □ cite□

That is what Jesus is telling Nicodemus: the Kingdom is not built by taking power; it is received by new birth.

God Loves the World

Finally, Jesus brings Nicodemus to the center:

“For God so loved the world that he gave his only begotten Son, that whoever bel...

Discussion Questions

1. Why does Jesus say the Kingdom must be *seen* through rebirth?
2. How does eternal life begin now rather than later?
3. Where do visible power structures distract from God's unseen Kingdom?

Chapter 18: The Samaritan Woman and Eternal Life

John 4:1-42

Jesus' conversation with the Samaritan woman follows immediately after his encounter with Nicodemus, and the contrast is intentional. Nicodemus was a Jewish man, a religious authority, and a respected teacher who came to Jesus under the cover of night. The Samaritan woman was none of these. She was a woman, a Samaritan, and socially vulnerable. She met Jesus in the open light of day, at the edge of society, while performing a daily task that marked her isolation.

John places these two encounters side by side to demonstrate that eternal life is not restricted by gender, ethnicity, religious pedigree, or moral reputation. Belief is offered to both the learned and the marginalized, but it takes shape differently in each life.

A Forbidden Conversation

Jesus was traveling north from Judea to Galilee and deliberately passed through Samaria—a region Jews normally avoided. The hostility between Jews and Samaritans stretched back centuries and was rooted in competing claims to land, Scripture, worship, and identity. Jews regarded Samaritans as ethnically impure and religiously compromised. Samaritans, in turn, rejected Jerusalem as the proper place of worship and centered their religious life on Mount Gerizim.

At Jacob's well, Jesus encountered a woman drawing water at noon. Her presence at that hour is telling. Women typically drew water in the cooler morning hours, together. Her isolation suggests social exclusion—confirmed later by Jesus' knowledge of her personal history.

When Jesus asked her for a drink, he violated multiple social taboos at once: a Jewish man speaking to a Samaritan woman, alone, about something as intimate as shared water. She immediately recognized the transgression and named it.

Jesus did not apologize. He redirected the conversation.

Living Water and Misunderstood Thirst

Jesus offered her "living water," a phrase that carried both literal and metaphorical meaning. At first, she heard only the literal sense—flowing water that would spare her daily labor. Jesus allowed the misunderstanding to stand briefly, then deepened it. The water he offered was not a convenience but a transformation: a source of life that would become internal, enduring, and self-renewing.

This exchange reveals something essential about belief in John's Gospel. Belief often begins with practical concerns—relief, help, survival—but Jesus consistently moves the conversation toward ultimate reality. He does not shame the woman for her misunderstanding. He leads her through it.

Truth Without Condemnation

When Jesus named her marital history, the conversation turned sharply personal. Yet his words carried no accusation. He did not label her immoral, nor did he demand repentance. He spoke truth without condemnation—and she recognized it immediately.

Her response is crucial: "Sir, I see that you are a prophet."

Truth, in John's Gospel, is not a weapon. It is a revelation that opens the possibility of life. The woman was not driven away by exposure; she was drawn closer by being known.

Worship Reframed

The woman shifted the conversation to worship—Jerusalem or Mount Gerizim. This was not deflection; it was theology. For Samaritans, worship location defined religious legitimacy.

Jesus' response dissolved the debate entirely. True worship, he explained, is no longer tied to place, ethnicity, or temple. It is defined by Spirit and truth. Access to God is no longer mediated by geography or heritage but by relationship.

This was a radical claim. It meant that neither Jewish nor Samaritan systems held ultimate authority. Eternal life was not inherited; it was received.

Belief and Revelation

When the woman spoke of the coming Messiah, Jesus made one of the clearest self-revelations in the Gospel: "I who speak to you am he."

Unlike Nicodemus, who struggled to grasp Jesus' meaning, the Samaritan woman responded with action. She left her water jar—the very reason she had come—and returned to her town. The symbol is unmistakable. Her old patterns of survival were interrupted by new life.

From Marginalized Woman to Communal Witness

The woman did not become a theologian or a moral exemplar. She became a witness. She told her community what had happened, and they came to see Jesus for themselves. Many believed—not because of her testimony alone, but because they encountered Jesus directly.

John records a remarkable outcome: a Samaritan village welcomed Jesus and confessed him as "the Savior of the world." This title moves far beyond Jewish messianic expectation. It is universal in scope and missional in vision.

Eternal Life Made Visible

This encounter reveals eternal life not as abstraction but as lived reality. The woman moved from isolation to community, from shame to agency, from exclusion to participation. Her life became a sign of the Kingdom that cannot be seen but can be experienced.

What Nicodemus struggled to understand at night, the Samaritan woman began to live out at noon. She was, in the deepest sense, born again.

Why This Story Matters for Mission

This chapter is not primarily about gender, ethnicity, or morality—though all are present. It is about how eternal life enters the world. It enters through encounter, truth spoken in love, and belief that reshapes identity and community.

For the believers in Ephesus—and for readers today—this story declared that no one is beyond the reach of life in Jesus. Eternal life begins where barriers fall and truth is received.

The Mother Arab Church

By the year 2000, using the broadest definition of Christian—those with full or partial Christian ancestry—the term *Palestinian Christian* encompassed an estimated 500,000 people worldwide. The overwhelming majority of Palestinian Christians identify as Arabs. According to the U.S. State Department's *International Religious Freedom Report* (2022), approximately 50,000 Christian Palestinians live in the West Bank and Jerusalem, with about 1,300 Arab Christians in Gaza. Others are citizens of Israel, and many more live in long-established diaspora communities across the Middle East and the West.

These Arab Christian communities live at the crossroads of faith, ethnicity, and political upheaval—conditions that have tested the church's witness in recent decades. One of the most severe trials followed the withdrawal of U.S. troops from Iraq in 2011, when the militant group ISIS swept across large areas of Iraq and Syria. Their goal was the violent establishment of an Islamic caliphate and the elimination of all who did not conform to their ideology.

Among those most brutally targeted were the Yazidis of northern Iraq and Syria, an ancient ethno-religious community long regarded as heretical by extremist clerics. Tensions between Yazidis, Kurds, and Arab Muslims—some stretching back centuries—collapsed into open violence. Mount Sinjar, the Yazidis' ancestral homeland near the Iraq–Syria border south of Türkiye, became the epicenter of catastrophe.

In 2014, ISIS attacked Sinjar. Thousands of Yazidi men were massacred, their bodies discarded in mass graves. Women and children were kidnapped and enslaved. According to the Iraqi Prime Minister, herself a Yazidi from Sinjar, 6,383 women and children were taken captive. By 2016, 2,590 had escaped, while 3,793 remained unaccounted for. Many others died from dehydration, untreated injuries, or exhaustion while fleeing.

In the midst of this devastation, the unseen Kingdom of God was quietly at work.

In 2016, an Arab pastor leading a Kurdish-speaking church in Duhok—about fifty miles north of Mosul—was compelled by the Spirit of God to begin humanitarian ministry among Yazidi refugees living in nearby camps. The Christian and Missionary Alliance, through its relief arm CAMA, asked me to visit him, learn what the church was doing, and explore how support might flow from U.S. churches through a partner congregation in Beirut, Lebanon.

My attempts to contact the Beirut pastor were unsuccessful—until God arranged an unexpected meeting.

That same year, the Alliance World Fellowship was convened in Bangkok. While traveling through Dubai with my wife, Connie, we sat beside an Arab man in a crowded waiting area. He asked if we were Americans, then if we were attending the AWF gathering. We soon realized we were colleagues in the same denomination.

"My name is Pastor M.D.," he said.

I replied, "You are the pastor of the Beirut church."

A shared personal history quickly emerged, confirming that this meeting was no coincidence.

Later in Bangkok, Pastor M.D. described how women dressed in black burkas—along with their children—had begun attending his church. He believed they were the families of ISIS fighters who had been killed or driven out. They had nowhere else to go.

"I tell them that Jesus loves them," he said. "I invite them to receive the gift of eternal life. I do not care if ISIS takes my head. These women and their families will be welcomed. If they choose to follow Jesus, they will join others who have made the same choice."

At the same moment in history, an Arab pastor in northern Iraq was ministering to victims of ISIS, while another Arab pastor in Beirut was ministering to the families of the perpetrators. This is the Kingdom you cannot see—breaking down walls of hatred, violence, and fear.

The Kingdom of God is not a political territory or ethnic stronghold. It is a spiritual reality that heals ancient wounds, dismantles prejudice, and makes reconciliation possible. From the woman at the well onward, the Arab church has borne witness to a Kingdom that welcomes the vulnerable, the outcast, and even enemies—offering eternal life that begins now, as we follow Jesus together.

Discussion Questions

1. Why does John contrast Nicodemus with the Samaritan woman?
2. How does Jesus reveal truth without condemnation?
3. What barriers still prevent marginalized voices from becoming witnessers?

Chapter 19: The Paralyzed Man at the Pool

John 5:1-30

After this there was a feast of the Jews, and Jesus went up to Jerusalem. Now there is in Jerusalem by the Sheep Gate a pool, in Aramaic called Bethesda, which has five roofed colonnades. In these lay a multitude of invalids—blind, lame, and paralyzed. One man was there who had been an invalid for thirty-eight years. When Jesus saw him lying there and knew that he had already been there a long time, he said to him, **"Do you want to be healed?"**

The sick man answered him, "Sir, I have no one to put me into the pool when the water is stirred up, and while I am going, another steps down before me."

Jesus said to him,

Get up, take up your bed, and walk."

And at once the man was healed, and he took up his bed and walked.

Now that day was the Sabbath. (John 5:1–9)

Do You Want to Be Healed?

Jesus' question is not naïve. It is diagnostic.

After thirty-eight years of paralysis, this man had learned how to survive without hope. His life revolved around waiting—waiting for movement in the water, waiting for someone to help him, waiting for something to change. Jesus did not ask, *"Do you deserve to be healed?"* or *"Have you suffered long enough?"* He asked whether the man was willing to reclaim agency, responsibility, and restored dominion over his life.

The man did not answer yes or no. Instead, he explained his system of survival. He had adapted to powerlessness.

Jesus responded not with sympathy, but with command: "Get up."

In that moment, eternal life broke into the present.

A World with No Place for the Disabled

For John's readers—especially those living in Ephesus—the scene at the Pool of Bethesda would have been tragically familiar. In the Roman world, there were no hospitals, no rehabilitation, and no meaningful medical care for the disabled. Physical impairment was often seen as fate, divine displeasure, or simply an unfortunate burden best left to the margins of society.

Disabled adults and exposed children were frequently left near temples, city gates, or public gathering places. Survival depended on almsgiving, superstition, or exploitation. Disability, sickness, and death were tightly linked—almost inevitable companions.

A letter discovered among the Oxyrhynchus Papyri illustrates how widespread abandonment was in the Roman world. A laborer named Hilarion wrote to his pregnant wife from Alexandria around 1 B.C., instructing her that if the child were male, she should keep it; if female, she should expose it. Such instructions were disturbingly ordinary.

Against this backdrop, the paralyzed man had likely been placed at Bethesda as a child or young adult. His entire life had unfolded within the confines of abandonment and waiting.

Get Up, Take Up Your Mat, and Walk

When Jesus healed the man, he restored more than mobility.

For the first time in nearly four decades, the man was no longer lying down. He was standing. The mat that once carried him followed him. This reversal is not incidental—it is symbolic.

Dominion had been restored.

Eternal life, as John presents it, is not merely future salvation. It is the recovery of agency now—the ability to participate in life as God intended. Jesus did not simply remove suffering; he returned responsibility, movement, and purpose.

The Sabbath Conflict

The healing took place on the Sabbath, and that is where the story turns confrontational.

The religious leaders were not outraged that a man had suffered for thirty-eight years. They were outraged that he carried his mat.

Their devotion to the law had eclipsed compassion. A system meant to protect life had become a structure that defended immobility. In guarding the Sabbath, they had forgotten its purpose.

Jesus did not break the Sabbath. He restored it.

"Sin No More" and Responsibility Restored

Later, Jesus found the man in the temple and said,

"See, you are well! Sin no more, that nothing worse may happen to you."

Jesus was not suggesting that paralysis had been caused by sin. Throughout the Gospels, he repeatedly rejects that logic. Rather, he was warning the man that restored life carries responsibility. Eternal life is not merely rescue from suffering—it is a call to live differently within

God's restored order. To return to patterns of dependency, injustice, or destructive behavior would be to surrender dominion once again.

Healing restores opportunity. How that opportunity is lived matters.

Law Versus Life

This incident exposed two irreconcilable visions of faith. One vision preserved order, tradition, and authority—even at the cost of human flourishing. The other restored life, dignity, and agency—even when it disrupted systems of control.

The religious leaders passed by suffering every day without seeing it. Jesus saw the man, met him, and changed his future.

Eternal Life Made Visible

This healing was not simply a miracle; it was a declaration.

A man once defined by waiting was now defined by movement. A life shaped by helplessness had been reclaimed. Eternal life had entered the present, restoring dominion where it had long been lost.

This is the Kingdom you cannot see—until it changes someone's life.

Discussion Questions

1. Why does Jesus ask, "Do you want to be healed?"

2. How can systems unintentionally preserve suffering?

3. What responsibilities come with restored life and agency?

Chapter 20: "I AM..."

John 6:1-59

The peak of Jesus' public ministry occurs in John chapter six, not because of political success or popular acclaim, but because human hunger collides with divine revelation.

A vast crowd followed Jesus into a remote place. They were far from home, far from markets, and far from provision. By late afternoon, hunger became unavoidable. Five loaves of bread and two small fish—offered by a young boy—were all that could be found. Jesus took that offering, gave thanks, and distributed it. Everyone ate. Everyone was satisfied. Twelve baskets of leftovers remained.

John is careful to show that this miracle was not random. It echoed Israel's story. As God once provided manna in the wilderness while leading His people from slavery toward promise, He now fed His people again in a desolate place. But this time, something greater was happening.

From Gift to Giver

After the meal, Jesus redirected attention from the miracle to its meaning. He said

"I AM the Bread of Life."

With those words, the focus shifted from the gift to the Giver, from temporary provision to eternal life. Manna sustained Israel for a day. Jesus offered life that endures.

The crowd wanted bread. Jesus offered Himself.

The Name That Reveals God

John's Gospel does something deliberate here. He does not allow Jesus to be understood merely as a miracle worker or moral teacher. He records seven moments where Jesus speaks words that unmistakably identify Him with the God of Israel.

To understand their weight, John's readers—especially Greek readers—had to look backward before they could look forward.

In Exodus 3, God spoke to Moses from the burning bush on the far side of the wilderness, near Horeb, the mountain of God. He revealed His concern for enslaved Israel:

"I have seen the misery of my people. I have heard their cries. I have come down to rescue them."

When Moses asked what name he should give Pharaoh, God answered:

"I AM that I AM. Tell them, 'I AM' has sent you."

"I AM" is not a description. It is a declaration of eternal existence. God does not become. He does not evolve. He does not depend. He simply *is*.

"I AM" led Israel out of slavery.
"I AM" parted the Red Sea.
"I AM" fed His people in the wilderness.
"I AM" guided them by fire and cloud.
"I AM" gave them land, law, and life.

A Radical Claim in a Greek World

This name would have sounded alien—even offensive—to Greek ears.

Greek religion was polytheistic and fragmented. The gods were many, limited, jealous, and flawed. They demanded appeasement, not relationship. They offered power, not transformation. They were bound by fate, rivalry, and time.

No Greek god could say, "I AM."

Greek gods existed *within* the world. Israel's God existed *before* it.

When Jesus spoke the words "I AM," He was not offering another deity to the pantheon. He was dismantling it.

The Seven "I AM" Declarations

John records seven moments when Jesus speaks this divine name:

I am the ***bread of life*** *(6:35)*

I am the ***light of the world*** *(8:12)*

I am the ***door*** *(10:7)*

I am the ***good shepherd*** *(10:11, 14)*

I am the ***resurrection and the life*** *(11:25)*

I am the ***way, the truth, and the life*** *(14:6)*

I am the ***true vine*** *(15:1)*

These are not abstractions. Each addresses a human loss: Hunger. Darkness. Exclusion. Fear. Death. Confusion. Disconnection. Jesus does not merely explain life—He restores it.

Restored Dominion and Eternal Life

In John's Gospel, eternal life is not postponed until death. It begins now.

To eat the Bread of Life is to recover dependence without degradation.
To follow the Light is to regain direction. To belong to the Shepherd is to live without fear. To abide in the Vine is to bear fruit again. This is restored dominion.

Life no longer controls us. Fear no longer governs us. Death no longer defines us.

The Spirit of Jesus flows through believers, empowering love, courage, obedience, and community. Eternal life is not escape from the world; it is transformation within it.

Why the Greeks Believed

The Greeks were not drawn to Jesus because He fit their myths. They believed because He shattered them.

Here was a God who entered suffering instead of exploiting it. Here was a God who fed the hungry rather than demanding sacrifice. Here was a God who gave life instead of bargaining for power. When Jesus said, "I AM," He was not making a philosophical claim. He was offering life. And many believed.

Closing Insight

The crowd wanted bread that would not run out. Jesus offered life that would not end. When one believes that Jesus is the Son of God, the great "I AM" leads the way—not only to eternal life in the future, but to restored dominion in the present.

Discussion Questions

1. Why are Jesus' "I AM" statements so central to John's Gospel?
2. Which human need addressed by these statements resonates most with you?
3. How does Jesus redefine dependence and abundance?

Chapter 21: The Adulterous Woman

John 8:2-11

Early in the morning, Jesus returned to the temple courts. The people gathered around Him, and He sat down to teach. As he spoke, the scribes and Pharisees dragged a woman into the open space before him.

"Teacher," they said, "this woman was caught in the act of adultery. In the Law, Moses commanded us to stone such women. What do you say?"

They were not seeking justice. They were setting a trap.

Jesus bent down and wrote with his finger on the ground. When they continued pressing him, he stood and said,

"Let the one who is without sin among you be the first to throw a stone."

Then he bent down again.

One by one, beginning with the oldest, they walked away.

Jesus was left alone with the woman. He asked,

"Woman," where are they? Has no one condemned you?"

"No one, Lord," she replied.

He replied,

"Neither do I condemn you,"

"Go, and from now on, sin no more."

A Public Trial, A Private Life

This story is about hypocritical religious men—and more.

We are right to be skeptical about how this woman was "caught in the act." Adultery requires two people, yet only the woman was exposed, humiliated, and threatened with death. The man was invisible. That silence reveals the deeper issue: a worldview that devalued women.

She was doubly abused, exploited, and then weaponized as a pawn in a public power struggle.

Women in the Ephesian World

John's readers in Ephesus would have recognized this scene at once.

Ephesian society offered women sharply divided roles. At one extreme stood the Temple of Artemis—one of the largest and wealthiest temples in the ancient world—where female priestesses and workers held respected religious positions. Artemis was associated with fertility, protection, and prosperity.

Yet this empowerment was narrow and conditional.

Just steps away from the Celsius Library stood a brothel, advertised openly in stone. Prostitution was legal, normalized, and often driven by economic desperation. Poor and enslaved women were especially vulnerable, valued for use rather than dignity.

The famous Greek statesman Demosthenes summarized the prevailing ethic bluntly:

"We have courtesans for pleasure, concubines for daily cohabitation, and wives for legitimate children and household management."

Women were defined by function, not by personhood.

John's story of the woman brought before Jesus would have struck Ephesian readers as painfully familiar.

Who Condemns You?

The Pharisees were not interested in the woman's guilt, innocence, or future. They were interested in control. If Jesus condemned her, he would affirm their authority. If he released her, they would accuse him of lawlessness.

Jesus chose a third way.

He did not deny the law, and he did not deny mercy. He exposed the hearts of the accusers.

When the stones fell to the ground, condemnation lost its power.

Neither Do I Condemn You

Jesus' words echo his earlier conversation with Nicodemus:

"God did not send his Son into the world to condemn the world, but to save the world through him."

Jesus did not publicly condemn the men either. That may seem unjust—until we realize that condemnation had already done its work. They judged themselves and left.

Condemnation strips people of dominion. It freezes them in the past and locks them into shame. Grace does the opposite.

Go, and Sin No More

Jesus did not excuse sin. He restored a future.

"Go, and sin no more" is not a threat; it is an invitation. For the first time, the woman was free to imagine a life not governed by exploitation, secrecy, or fear.

This is eternal life experienced in the present.

Rwanda: When Condemnation Failed

After the 1994 genocide, Rwanda faced a devastating HIV/AIDS epidemic. By 2002, roughly eight percent of the population was infected. The disease spread quietly for years, amplified by stigma and silence.

Many believed AIDS was punishment. Churches avoided the subject. Condemnation filled the pulpits, and truth retreated into darkness.

Then reality forced a reckoning. Pastor Bizimana stood before his congregation after burying yet another young person and said:

"A few years ago, we thought AIDS was far from us. Today it is in our families, our churches, and our schools. We must wake up."

The church faced a choice—continue condemning or begin healing.

Grace Creates Change

With help from World Relief, pastors across Rwanda learned how to speak truth without shame, how to teach about sexuality responsibly, how to care for the sick, widows, and orphans, and how to replace silence with compassion.

Ministry shifted from condemnation to grace. That change saved lives.

Like the woman in John 8, people could finally step out of hiding. Dominion—over health, relationships, and future—began to return.

Law or Life

The Pharisees cared about the law, not the woman's life. The church in Rwanda learned that condemnation preserves appearances but destroys people. Grace tells the truth and opens a future. Jesus' response in John 8 is not permissive. It is redemptive.

Eternal Life Now

The woman stood trapped in a life she could not escape. Jesus did not deny her past—but he refused to let it define her future.

This is how Jesus changes the world.

Eternal life is not merely a promise after death. It is the restoration of dignity, agency, and hope **now**. And it begins when condemnation ends and grace and redemption begin.

Discussion Questions

1. How does condemnation strip people of dominion?
2. Why does Jesus combine grace with responsibility?
3. How can the Church model truth without shame today?

Chapter 22: The Blind Man

John 9:1-41

In chapter nine of John's Gospel, Jesus meets the fifth individual in our unfolding series of encounters. This story is not only about a man receiving physical sight; it is about a world being challenged to see differently.

From this encounter, the disciples learn something new about eternal life, a blind man finds his voice and articulates belief, and religious leaders are exposed for their spiritual blindness.

Who Is to Blame?

As Jesus passed by, he saw a man who had been blind from birth. His disciples asked a question that revealed far more about themselves than about the man:

"Rabbi, who sinned, this man or his parents, that he was born blind?"

Their question assumed that suffering must have a moral cause.

Jesus rejected the premise entirely.

"Neither this man nor his parents sinned," he replied, "but this happened so that the works of God might be displayed in him."

With that statement, Jesus dismantled a worldview shared by both Jews and Greeks.

Blindness as Judgment?

In the ancient world, sickness and disability were widely interpreted as punishment or curse.

Greek culture viewed illness as the result of offending the gods or failing moral tests. Hebrew tradition, shaped in part by Deuteronomy, often associated obedience with blessing and disobedience with curse. Over time, this theology hardened into a justification for neglect.

If illness was deserved, responsibility disappeared. Jesus refused that logic.

If blindness was not fate or punishment, then responsibility for care, compassion, and healing returned to the community.

Light in the World

Jesus continued:

"As long as I am in the world, I am the light of the world."

Then He acted. He made mud, anointed the man's eyes, and sent him to wash in the Pool of Siloam—Sent. The man went, washed, and came back seeing.

This was not merely a miracle. It was a declaration that darkness—physical and spiritual—does not have the final word.

I Am the Man

The neighbors were confused. "Isn't this the man who used to sit and beg?"

Some said yes. Others doubted. The healed man answered with simple clarity: "I am the man."

For the first time in his life, he was not defined by disability or dependency. Seeing restored his agency. His future was no longer predetermined. This is restored dominion.

Conflict Creates Clarity

Ironically, belief did not arise immediately from healing. It emerged through resistance. The Pharisees could not celebrate what God had done because it violated their categories. Healing on the Sabbath was labeled "work." Law was elevated above life.

Their refusal to see pushed the man forward. "I was blind," he said, "but now I see." And in seeing, he came to believe that Jesus was Lord.

Narcissus and the Failure to See

John's Ephesian readers would have recognized this blindness from their own culture.

The Greek myth of Narcissus tells of a man incapable of seeing others. He rejected love, showed no empathy, and became consumed by his reflection. His punishment was endless self-absorption.

The Greeks could diagnose the disease—but they had no cure. Jesus offers one.

Learning to See

Culture teaches us how to see—or not.

David Brooks, reflecting on art and memory, reminds us that great works do not lecture; they reveal. Museums that preserve the horror of Auschwitz or the history of lynching in America force us to imagine lives we might otherwise ignore. Art awakens empathy. Memory disrupts denial.

Seeing reshapes conscience. Jesus accused the Pharisees of choosing not to see. They walked the same streets as the blind beggar. They passed suffering daily. Yet they preserved the status quo through legalism. It takes effort to remain blind.

A New Future Opened

When Jesus met Nicodemus, the paralytic, the woman caught in adultery, and the blind man, he did not make them wealthy or immune to future hardship. He did something more profound. He opened futures that were previously closed.

The blind man could now imagine a life of participation, contribution, and dignity. Eternal life had begun as escape from the world, but as restored engagement within it.

Seeing as Realized Eschatology

John's Gospel presents realized eschatology: the present experience of future life. A little of heaven now. To see the world as God intends it—and to act accordingly—is to live eternal life in the present. Jesus modeled a new kind of leadership: responsibility for human flourishing, not preservation of privilege.

This was unfamiliar to the Pharisees. It is still unfamiliar to many today. But this is how Jesus changes the world—by teaching us to see.

Discussion Questions

1. Why does Jesus reject the idea that suffering is caused by personal sin?
2. How does physical sight lead to spiritual clarity?
3. Where might we be choosing not to see suffering around us?

Chapter 23: Lazarus

John 11:1-44

John chapter eleven marks the end of Jesus' public ministry and forms the decisive bridge to his suffering, trial, and crucifixion. In this chapter, Jesus confronts the final and greatest enemy of humanity—not sickness, not sin, but death itself.

The Delay That Reveals Glory

Lazarus, a close friend of Jesus, fell gravely ill in Bethany, the village where his sisters Mary and Martha lived. They sent word to Jesus: "Lord, the one you love is ill."

Jesus' response was startling:
"This illness does not lead to death. It is for the glory of God, so that the Son of God may be glorified through it."

John immediately adds an important clarification: Jesus loved Martha, her sister, and Lazarus. Love, not indifference, shaped what followed.

Instead of leaving immediately, Jesus waited two more days. Only then did he tell his disciples,

"Let us go to Judea again."

This delay was deliberate. It ensured that Lazarus was unquestionably dead. No coma. No ambiguity. No hope left in human terms.

Facing Death Head-On

By the time Jesus arrived, Lazarus had been in the tomb four days. In first-century Jewish understanding, decomposition had already begun. Death was final.

> Now Jesus loved Martha and her sister and Lazarus. So, when he heard that Lazarus was ill, he stayed two days longer in the place where he was. Then, after this, he said to the disciples,
>
> "*Let us go to Judea again."*
>
> The disciples said to him, "Rabbi, the Jews were just now seeking to stone you, and are you going there again?" Jesus answered,

Are there not twelve hours in the day? If anyone walks in the day, he does not stumble, because he sees the light of this world. However, if anyone walks in the night, he stumbles, because the light is not in him." After saying these things, he said to them, "Our friend Lazarus has fallen asleep, but I go to awaken him." The disciples said to him, "Lord, if he has fallen asleep, he will recover." Now Jesus had spoken of his death, but they thought that he meant taking rest in sleep. Then Jesus told them plainly, "Lazarus has died, and for your sake I am glad that I was not there, so that you may believe. But let us go to him." So, Thomas, called the Twin, said to his fellow disciples, "Let us also go, that we may die with him" (Jn. 11:1-16).

Martha met Jesus outside the village. Her words carried both faith and grief: "Lord, if you had been here, my brother would not have died. But even now I know that whatever you ask from God, God will give you."

Jesus replied,

Your brother will rise again."

Martha answered with orthodox belief: "I know that he will rise again in the resurrection on the last day."

Jesus then moved the conversation from doctrine to identity:

"I am the resurrection and the life. Whoever believes in me, though he die, yet he live, and everyone who lives and believes in me shall never die. Do you believe this?"

Martha's confession stands among the clearest in the Gospel: "Yes, Lord; I believe that you are the Christ, the Son of God, who is coming into the world."

After this conversation, Martha returned and quietly told her sister Mary, "The Teacher is here and is calling for you." When Mary heard this, she rose quickly and went to him. Jesus had not yet entered the village but was still at the place where Martha had met him. Seeing Mary leave so abruptly the Jews who were consoling her followed, assuming she was going to the tomb to weep there.

When Mary reached Jesus and saw him, she fell at his feet and said, "Lord, if you had been here, my brother would not have died." When Jesus saw her weeping—and the others who came with her also weeping—he was deeply moved in spirit and troubled. He asked,

"Where have you laid him?"

They replied, "Lord, come and see."

Jesus wept.

Some who saw this said, "See how he loved him." Others, however, asked skeptically, "Could not the one who opened the eyes of the blind man have kept this man from dying?"

Jesus Raises Lazarus

Still deeply moved, Jesus came to the tomb. It was a cave, with a stone laid across the entrance. He said,

"Take away the stone,"

Martha, ever practical, objected. "Lord, by this time there will be an odor, for he has been dead four days."

Jesus replied,

Did I not tell you that if you believed, you would see the glory of God?"

So, they removed the stone. Jesus lifted his eyes and prayed aloud, not for his own sake, but for those standing nearby:

"Father, I thank you that you have heard me. I know that you always hear me, but I say this so that they may believe that you sent me."

Then he cried out with a loud voice,

"Lazarus, come out."

The man who had been dead came out—his hands and feet bound with linen strips; his face wrapped in cloth. Jesus said to them,

Unbind him and let him go."

Jesus did not have to meet with Nicodemus or the troubled woman at the well. He did not have to stop at the pool of Bethesda, where disabled people waited for healing. He could have ignored the Pharisees who challenged him with the woman caught in adultery. No one compelled him to seek out the blind man begging in the temple. And he certainly did not have to come to the home of Mary and Martha four days after Lazarus had died.

Yet if Jesus had limited his ministry to religious debates, moral instruction, compassionate words, or even physical healings, we might remember him as a wise teacher or prophet.

But that was not his mission.

If he had answered our spiritual questions, corrected our theology, and healed our bodies—but avoided the problem of death itself—he would have failed to confront humanity's deepest fear. There was a deliberate pattern in Jesus' ministry: he sought out humanity's most intractable problems and pointed a way through them. The final and greatest enemy was death. That is why he is remembered.

At the end of the first century, death was a constant presence. Children died at birth or were abandoned. Adults were carried off by disease. Life was fragile and brief. Everyone lived under the shadow of *bios*—inevitable decline ending in death.

Jesus delayed going to Lazarus precisely so there would be no doubt. Lazarus was not asleep. He was conscious. He was dead—and had been long enough for decay to begin. Mary and Martha knew it. The mourners knew it. Death was undeniable.

Lazarus' death and resurrection foreshadowed Jesus' own—and ours. His raising was not a denial of death's reality, but a declaration that death does not have the final word. What Jesus revealed was that eternal life does not begin after death; it begins before it.

Earlier, Jesus had said,

"I am the resurrection and the life. The one who believes in me will live, even though they die, and whoever lives by believing in me will never die.

This is eternal life: not merely endless existence in the future, but a transformed quality of life in the present that continues beyond death. As John later defines it, eternal life is.

… *"knowing you, the only true God, and Jesus Christ, whom you have sent."*

That day, Jesus called a dead man from an underground tomb, and Lazarus walked out alive. It was a sign—just as Nicodemus had once recognized. Because Jesus is the Son of God, those who believe in him possess a life that overcomes death. This is the worldview John called the Ephesians—and all his readers—to believe.

Discussion Questions

1. Why does Jesus delay before acting—and what does that reveal?
2. How does this story redefine death and hope?
3. What does it mean to believe before seeing outcomes?

Part III

Good News for Our Time

Chapter 24: In The Upper Room

John 12-17

As Jesus rode a donkey through Jerusalem's gate, crowds surged around him, shouting and laying palm branches before him—the welcome reserved for a conquering king. News of Lazarus rising from the dead had electrified the city. Pilgrims arriving for Passover swelled the streets, and messianic expectation reached a fever pitch.

The religious leaders saw the danger clearly. They had failed to silence Jesus through debate or intimidation. Now they concluded that something decisive had to be done. "The whole world is going after him," they said. Quietly, they began to plan his death.

Roman authorities were uneasy as well. Judea had a long history of rebellion. Messianic figures had repeatedly ignited uprisings, and Rome crushed them without mercy. From their perspective, Jesus looked like another charismatic leader riding a wave of popular enthusiasm—one capable of destabilizing the fragile peace.

Everyone sensed that something was about to break.

The Final Hours

In the hours before his arrest, Jesus withdrew with his disciples to an upper room. The mood was contradictory excitement mixed with dread. The disciples still imagined political restoration and argued about who would hold positions of authority in the coming kingdom. Yet only the night before, Jesus had spoken openly about his death. Opposition was intensifying. Betrayal was already in motion.

Mary of Bethany had anointed Jesus' feet with oil—an unmistakable act of preparation for burial. Still, the disciples clung to their assumptions. Three years with Jesus had not yet dismantled their vision of power.

Jesus knew this moment required something more radical than explanation.

A Kingdom Turned Upside Down

As the disciples debated greatness, Jesus stopped them and said:

"The kings of the Gentiles exercise lordship over them… But not so with you. Rather, the greatest among you must become like the youngest, and the leader like one who serves. I am among you as one who serves." (Luke 22:25–27)

Then he did what no one expected. Jesus wrapped a towel around his waist and began to wash his disciples' feet—an act reserved for servants and enslaved people.

For readers in Ephesus, this scene would have been stunning. In Greek and Roman culture, honor flowed downward. Worth was measured by status. The powerful were served; the weak served. Here, the pattern was reversed. The Lord became the servant.

The Meaning of the Towel

Foot washing was not symbolic humility—it was embodied inversion. By kneeling before his disciples, Jesus dismantled the hierarchy that governed every known kingdom. Where social position determined value, Jesus declared that service restores dignity. By humbling himself, he elevated others. When he finished, he said:

"You call me Teacher and Lord—and rightly so. Now that I, your Lord and Teacher, have washed your feet, you also should wash one another's feet… I have given you an example." (John 13:13–15)

This was not a ritual to admire. It was a way of life to practice.

What If We Lived This Way?

If people washed one another's feet—literally or figuratively—the consequences would be revolutionary.

- Power would become responsibility.
- Leadership would become service.
- Status would lose its grip.
- The vulnerable would be seen.
- Dignity would be restored.

This is what restored dominion looks like in community. Eternal life, as Jesus describes it, is not escape from the world. It is a reordering of the world around love.

"In My Father's House"

Knowing fear would soon overwhelm them, Jesus spoke words of reassurance:

"Do not let your hearts be troubled. Believe in God; believe also in me. In my Father's house are many rooms… I go to prepare a place for you." (John 14:1–2)

"In my Father's house" is family language. It assures belonging, not geography. Jesus was not abandoning them—he was securing their place within God's household. When Thomas asked, "How can we know the way?" Jesus answered:

"I am the way, the truth, and the life."

For Greek readers accustomed to many "ways" of wisdom, Jesus made an exclusive yet relational claim: eternal life is found not in ideas, but in following him.

The Gift of Presence

Jesus then promised what would make this way possible—the Holy Spirit. Unlike the impersonal spirits of Greek mythology, the Holy Spirit is God's personal presence: Counselor, Advocate, Comforter, Spirit of Truth. The Spirit would not replace Jesus' teaching but extend it—dwelling within believers.

Jesus would no longer walk beside them. He would live in them.

A Prayer for the World

Finally, Jesus prayed—not for escape from suffering, but for faithfulness within it.

He asked the Father to protect his followers, to fill them with joy, and to sustain them in a world that would misunderstand and oppose them. He prayed not only for those in the room, but for all who would believe in their witness. This is eternal life lived under pressure.

Dominion Reimagined

The Upper Room reveals what the Kingdom looks like after Jesus' departure:

- Authority exercised through service
- Truth embodied in love

- Power expressed as sacrifice
- Life shared, not controlled.

This is not weakness. It is the strongest force the world has ever known. Believing Jesus is the Son of God—following his way, learning his truth, and receiving his life—is the present experience of future eternal life.

And it begins with a towel.

Discussion Questions

1. Why does Jesus redefine leadership through service?
2. How does the foot-washing challenge modern power structures?
3. What would change if Christian communities lived this way?

Chapter 25: Betrayal to Resurrection

John 18-19

The tragedy that led to Jesus' execution began in the Garden of Gethsemane, east of the Kidron Valley on the slopes of the Mount of Olives, across from the Temple Mount in Jerusalem. It was a familiar place—one where Jesus often met with His disciples. Knowing this, Judas led a detachment of soldiers to arrest Him there.

In a moment of instinctive defense, Peter drew his sword and struck one of the soldiers, severing his ear—likely a failed attempt to take his life. What could have erupted into a massacre—eleven fishers, untrained in warfare, facing a band of soldiers and officers from the chief priests and Pharisees—was halted by an act of astonishing mercy. Jesus intervened, touched the wounded man, and healed him.

Peter's natural human instinct—*bios*, driven by fear and survival—would have unleashed devastating violence. Jesus' response revealed something entirely different. By healing His enemy, He demonstrated the nature of zoe—eternal life expressed through self-giving love, restraint, and restoration.

Betrayal

History is filled with betrayals that altered the course of nations and lives. Members of the Roman Senate assassinated Julius Caesar. Anne Boleyn was betrayed by King Henry VIII, her husband. Benedict Arnold betrayed the American colonies. Each of these acts reshaped history.

Yet the betrayal of Jesus stands apart. It set the worst of humanity's instincts against humanity's very best.

Betrayal was the original wound of Holy Week.

Betrayal arises from many motives: self-interest, fear, pressure, or the prioritizing of personal gain over loyalty and truth. It is a window into the soul where the ego seeks control, power, and validation. When ego dominates, people justify betraying those closest to them in order to preserve identity, gain advantage, or avoid vulnerability—even while their soul longs for connection and truth.

The dictionary defines betrayal as to give over, hand over, or delivering up. These are outward actions that reveal an inward disorder—a heart shaped by anger, envy, greed, fear, or resentment. Betrayal silences courage and compassion, replacing them with desperate attempts at self-preservation. It chooses illusion over truth, gain over integrity.

A lack of empathy allows betrayers to minimize the damage they cause. The promise of money, power, or control can make betrayal feel irresistible—even when it destroys the bonds of trust with a friend, a spouse, a leader, or a child.

Sometimes betrayal is calculated and deliberate. At other times, it flows from weakness, confusion, or the tragic belief that one is doing what is right. Regardless of motive, its consequences are profound. Trust, once broken, is nearly impossible to restore. Guilt often lingers for a lifetime. Relationships are lost, reputations damaged, and the betrayer is left isolated surrounded by people who neither trust nor respect them.

The long-term cost of betrayal always outweighs any short-term gain.

Betrayal is the most intimate and devastating of sins because it comes from within the circle of trust. It wounds the heart, not just the body. It breaks covenant—between friends, lovers, families, and ultimately, between humanity and God.

In Gethsemane, Jesus did not face death alone. He faced abandonment. Judas sold his knowledge of Jesus' place of prayer for thirty pieces of silver. Peter denied Him three times. The remaining disciples fled. The sting was not merely that Jesus was forsaken—but that He was forsaken by those He had chosen, loved, and formed.

It was a friend who greeted Him with a kiss while handing Him over to death. It was denial in the courtyard and silence at the cross. Betrayal is spiritually devastating because it is personal. It reflects a fractured covenant and a broken love.

Was Judas driven by greed, disappointment, or ideological disillusionment? Scripture does not fully answer that question. What it does reveal is the outcome. Judas embodied *bios*—decline and death. Matthew records that Judas confessed, "I have betrayed innocent blood," and then went out and took his own life (Matthew 27:5).

Crucifixion

Jesus' trials before Caiaphas and Pilate produced contradictory testimony and unsubstantiated accusations. Yet both religious and civil authorities agreed on one thing: Jesus posed a threat—to religious control and to Roman order.

Pilate sentenced Jesus to die by crucifixion. But death alone was not enough. He was beaten, mocked, and scourged. Then He was forced to carry His cross to the place of execution.

To the ancient Greeks, crucifixion was a brutal and degrading punishment—so shameful that it was rarely practiced among them. Cicero called it "a cruel and disgusting punishment" and argued it should never even be mentioned among civilized people.

The Apostle Paul acknowledged this cultural revulsion when he wrote, "the message of the cross is foolishness to those who are perishing" (1 Corinthians 1:18). For Greeks steeped in philosophy, rhetoric, and ideals of strength, the idea of a divine Savior dying a powerless, humiliating death was irrational and offensive.

In Greek and Roman thought, gods were powerful and immortal. They might suffer wounds, but they were never defeated, certainly never executed. A god who willingly submitted to death, especially such a horrific one, was incomprehensible.

Crucifixion was designed not only to kill but to humiliate. It was reserved for slaves, rebels, and non-citizens. In a culture that equated divinity with dominance, the idea that God would "empty himself, taking the form of a slave" was revolutionary.

Public executions were spectacles of terror. Victims were tortured in full view—so crowds could hear their cries, see their suffering, and imagine themselves on the cross. Like lynchings, crucifixions were meant to suppress hope and crush resistance.

While one individual suffered, the true target was the watching population.

In this light, Jesus' death stands as a profound substitution—not only for individual sin, but for all who are crushed by religious oppression, political domination, or the self-inflicted bondage of sin. The cross exposes the violence of *bios* and reveals the self-giving power of zoe—a life that overcomes death not by force, but by love.

Discussion Questions

1. How does betrayal expose the contrast between bios and zoe?
2. Why does Jesus refuse violence even in self-defense?
3. What does the cross reveal about power, love, and victory?

Chapter 26: The Resurrection and Appearances

John 20

In the Greek world—shaping the cultural and religious imagination of cities such as Ephesus—the afterlife was most commonly associated with the Underworld ruled by Hades. Human existence beyond death was understood as a shadowy, diminished continuation of life rather than a renewed, embodied existence. Resurrection had no meaningful place in Greek religious narratives.

Greek philosophers reinforced this outlook. Plato emphasized the immortality of the soul rather than the resurrection of the body, viewing the physical body as a temporary prison from which the soul should ultimately be freed. He speculated about cycles of purification and post-mortem existence, but not permanent bodily restoration. Epicurus went further, rejecting any form of afterlife altogether, arguing that death marked the complete end of consciousness and personal existence. The Stoics, for their part, focused on ethical living in harmony with nature and the divine order; while some allowed for a temporary survival of the soul, they placed little emphasis on personal resurrection or enduring life after death.

Against this intellectual and religious backdrop, the Christian proclamation of Jesus' bodily resurrection would have sounded implausible—if not offensive—to many Greeks. The idea that a physical body could be restored to life contradicted deeply held philosophical assumptions about the nature of reality, the soul, and the purpose of existence.

Yet the early Christian message rested not on philosophy but on claimed historical events.

On the third day after Jesus' crucifixion, women who had followed Him went to the tomb where His body had been laid, intending to anoint it with spices. When they arrived, they found the stone rolled away and the tomb empty. Alarmed and confused, Mary Magdalene ran to tell the disciples.

Peter and John rushed to the tomb and confirmed that it was empty. Though they did not yet fully understand the Scriptures that foretold the Messiah's resurrection, the reality of the empty tomb confronted them directly. Afterward, they returned to the others to report what they had seen.

Mary remained behind, weeping. It was there, outside the tomb, that the risen Jesus first appeared—to her. Mistaking Him for the gardener, she did not recognize Him until He spoke her name. At that moment, she realized that He was alive; risen from the dead.

Later that same day, Jesus appeared to two disciples traveling to the village of Emmaus, revealing Himself as they walked and explained the Scriptures. That evening, He appeared to the disciples gathered in Jerusalem, speaking with them and eating in their presence, transforming their fear and doubt into faith. One week later, He appeared again—this time with Thomas present—who believed when he saw the wounds in Jesus' hands and side.

In the days that followed, Jesus also appeared privately to Peter and to James. John records three distinct post resurrection appearances: twice in the upper room and once by the Sea of Galilee. Luke adds that

Jesus appeared repeatedly over a period of days, and Paul later testifies that He was seen by more than five hundred people at one time.

All of this took place within a thoroughly Greek cultural environment—yet with a striking difference. The gods of Greek mythology never appeared bodily alive to historical witnesses, never ate with followers, never bore wounds, and never conquered death. The resurrection of Jesus stood apart as a radically new claim: not myth, not metaphor, but an event that reshaped history and human hope.

Discussion Questions

1. Why was resurrection such a challenge to Greek thinking?
2. How does bodily resurrection change the meaning of eternal life?
3. What fears lose their power if resurrection is true?

Chapter 27: Feed My Sheep

John 21

John chapter 21 closes the Gospel by recounting a breakfast of grilled fish shared by Jesus and His disciples beside the Sea of Galilee. The men had fished throughout the night and caught nothing. At daybreak Jesus appeared on the shore and instructed them to cast their nets on the opposite side of the boat. In obedience to His word, they did so, and the nets were nearly torn apart by the overwhelming number of fish.

After the catch was secured, the disciples gathered around a charcoal fire where Jesus had prepared breakfast. As they ate, Jesus turned to Peter and asked a question that reached far beyond that quiet morning: "Do you love me more than these?"

The Greek word translated "these" is plural and can refer either to people or to things. It may have pointed to the other disciples gathered around the fire, to the fish they had just eaten, or—by implication—to Peter's former livelihood as a fisher. Each possibility touches a different dimension of Peter's loyalty and commitment.

Jesus asked Peter twice, "Do you love me?" using the verb *agapaō*. Peter responded each time, "You know that I love you," using the verb *phileō*. The third time Jesus asked the question, He adopted Peter's language: "Do you love (*phileō*) me?" This change wounded Peter, who replied, "Lord, you know all things; you know that I love you."

Strong's Concordance distinguishes these two words carefully. *Phileō* refers to affection, friendship, or fondness toward a person or object. *Agapaō,* by contrast, conveys a fuller and more deliberate love—one that involves judgment, commitment, and the assent of the will as a matter of principle and devotion. Jesus was asking Peter whether he loved Him wholly, with both heart and mind.

This fuller meaning echoes Jesus' earlier teaching when a teacher of the law asked, "What must I do to inherit eternal life?" Jesus answered, "Love the Lord your God with all your heart and with all your soul and with all your strength and with all.

Discussion Questions

1. Why was resurrection such a challenge to Greek thinking?
2. How does bodily resurrection change the meaning of eternal life?
3. What fears lose their power if resurrection is true?

Chapter 28: Good News for Our Time

We Need a Resurrection

The Gospel of John is about Jesus—from beginning to end. It is about grace given to ordinary people and revealed through extraordinary love.

Jesus turned water into wine at a village wedding. He spoke with a Samaritan woman rejected by her community. He healed a disabled man at Bethesda, rescued a woman caught in adultery, restored sight to a blind man in the Temple, and raised Lazarus from the dead. These signs reveal his divinity, but they also reveal something else: the vulnerable were the primary recipients of his grace.

Jesus could have displayed his power among the influential and admired. Instead, he chose the overlooked, the marginalized, and the wounded. John's Gospel is not merely about what Jesus did—it is about *who He is.*

A Gospel for the World

John wrote with cross-cultural clarity. He understood Greek philosophy, language, and religious imagination, and he spoke within that framework without surrendering the Jewish roots of Jesus' identity. He communicated truth without syncretism.

John also teaches ***r*ealized eschatology**: eternal life begins **now**. When one believes that Jesus is the Son of God, real life starts on earth. The invisible Kingdom becomes visible. Healing and wholeness become possible. Freedom from sin becomes attainable. Even death loses its final word.

Chapters 12–21 show how to live in the world after Jesus' ascension: practice humility, follow his way, live in truth, and share his life.

Humanity Revealed—and Redeemed

Under Pilate and Caiaphas, the crucifixion exposed how far humanity had fallen from its original design. The resurrection reveals God's intent for restoration.

Under Emperor Domitian, Greek readers saw themselves reflected in the Gospel—not morally superior to earlier Jewish leaders, but equally capable of exploiting religion, fostering injustice, neglecting the vulnerable, and failing to overcome death.

Despite their philosophical brilliance, the Greeks could not escape mortality.

They needed a resurrection.

We Need a Resurrection

When religion becomes politics and politics turns violent, we need a resurrection.
When truth is dismissed, lies are normalized, and trust collapses, we need a resurrection.
When children, the disabled, and the vulnerable wait unseen while the resourced look away, we need a resurrection.

We do not need better metaphors, grand monuments, deeper pockets, or more impressive idols. We do not need more self-congratulating leaders or lifeless ideals.

We need a resurrection.

We need empathy for the smallest and farthest away.

We need justice shaped by compassion.

We need redemption that reaches body, soul, and society.

We need God to reassemble lifeless molecules, restart silent hearts, refill empty lungs, and overcome death with the Breath of Life.

Thanks be to God—the risen Jesus lives among us by his Spirit.

The Power of the Resurrection

The apostle Paul explained the theological meaning of the cross and resurrection. John dares us to believe in a transformed future on earth.

The resurrection reshaped humanity's moral imagination. It declared that truth cannot be killed, justice cannot be crucified, and love—sacrificial love—is the most powerful force in the universe.

The living Jesus calls us to believe that his unseen Kingdom can unite all people under the banner of love.

We Have a Resurrection

Mary stood alone outside the empty tomb, exhausted and grieving—until Jesus spoke her name.

"I have seen the Lord," she said.

The disciples said, "We have seen the Lord."
Thomas said, "My Lord and my God."

Fear gave way to joy. Despair gave way to belief. The future opened.

Remove the fear of death, and tyrants lose their leverage. Remove the fear of death, and people gain courage to pursue freedom, justice, and life. This is the power of the Good News.

Life from the Inside Out

Jesus' resurrection released the Holy Spirit into the world. Knowledge works from the outside in. The Spirit works from the inside out.

The Spirit teaches, guides, heals, and reshapes hearts. He awakens believers to life in a new Kingdom—one marked by love, grace, hospitality, generosity, and care for the marginalized.

Early Christians understood themselves as part of a new creation, raised with Christ. This was the Kingdom of God made visible.

The Ongoing Impact

The impact of Jesus' resurrection continues today. Christianity's global reach, its influence on moral systems, law, history, and even our calendar trace back to one empty tomb.

Jesus of Nazareth remains the most consequential figure of the past two millennia.

When believers ask, "What would Jesus do?" they echo Mary's first proclamation: He is alive.

Why John Wrote

John concludes his Gospel with purpose and invitation:

*"I write these things so that you may believe that Jesus is the Christ, the Son of God, and that by believing you may have life in His Name.

This is how Jesus changes the world.

Discussion Questions

1. Why does the world still "need a resurrection?
2. How does the resurrection reshape justice, compassion, and hope?
3. What would it look like to live resurrection life in public and private spaces?
4.

Acknowledgements

One cannot author a book of any length without realizing the contributions and influences accumulated over a lifetime from family, friends, and mentors. Pastor Carmen McEwen, of the Malone Wesleyan Church and Dr. Morris Irvin, Pastor at Simpson Memorial Church in Nyack, New York, were early influences in my life and inspired me to pursue Christian ministry. Mr. and Mrs. Fajar, their son Setiawan, Mr. Marjono, and especially Mr. Sutaji, who whispered corrections to my Indonesian language in my ear while riding on the back of my motorcycle, helped me see what it is like to live as a follower of Jesus in a society as an oppressed minority. I am thankful to Dr. Yakob Tomatala who advised me on the sections of the book that relate to Indonesia.

I am indebted to Jean-Paul Ndagijimana, Gibson Nkanaunena, Dennis Mwangwela, and Dr. Pieter Ernst of World Relief who incarnate the ministry of Jesus as they confront poverty manifested in hunger, HIV/AIDS, infant mortality, and lack of access to capital for the poor in Africa.

Dr. David Klopfenstein, Dr. Jim Kovalik, and I spent hours in conversation in the gazebo by the pond in Good Samaritan Village in Kissimmee, Florida. Our talks were inspirational, corrective, and motivating, encouraging me to embark on this writing project.

Brad Eichhorn volunteered to proofread my text and offer formatting suggestions. What a generous offer! Brad's attention to detail was just what I needed. Thank you, Brad, your help was invaluable and an answer to prayer.

Above all, thank you, Connie, my loving, patient wife, for your helpful editing. Although I have written in the first person, everything alluded to in this book, we experienced and evaluated together. I am blessed to have traveled this journey of life with you.

While I have received help from generous friends, all the remaining errors are mine.

Gary Fairchild

Works Cited

(Sources directly referenced in footnotes)

Brooks, David. The Second Mountain: The Quest for a Moral Life. New York: Random House, 2019.

Byrne, Thomas. "False Profits: Reviving the Corporation's Public Purpose." UCLA Law Review (2010).

CAMA Services. "Hands of Honor." Accessed March 14, 2026. https://www.camaservices.org.

CAMA Services. "Health and Fitness for Kosovo." Accessed March 14, 2026. https://www.camaservices.org.

Ferngren, Gary B. "A New Era in Roman Healthcare." Christian History (2011). https://christianhistoryinstitute.org/magazine/article/new-era-in-roman-healthcare.

Hoffman, Martin J. "Prophecy and Fulfillment in the Old and New Testaments." Journal of Biblical Studies (1841–44).

Ladd, George Eldon. A Theology of the New Testament. Grand Rapids, MI: Eerdmans, 1974.

Lewis, C. S. Mere Christianity. New York: HarperOne, 1952.

Liddell, Henry George, Robert Scott, and Henry Stuart Jones. A Greek–English Lexicon. Clarendon Press, Oxford 1940.

Mayo Clinic Staff. "Narcissistic Personality Disorder." Mayo Clinic. Accessed March 14, 2026. https://www.mayoclinic.org.

Myers, Bryant L. Walking with the Poor: Principles and Practices of Transformational Development. Maryknoll, NY: Orbis Books, 1999.

Strong, James. Strong's Exhaustive Concordance of the Bible.

U.S. Department of State. International Religious Freedom Report. Accessed March 14, 2026. https://www.state.gov/religiousfreedomreport/.

Weber, Max. Economy, and Society. Translated by Guenther Roth and Claus Wittich. Berkeley: University of California Press, 1978.

Yeshiva.org. "Who Is an Am Ha'aretz?" Accessed March 14, 2026. https://www.yeshiva.org.

Works Consulted

(Formative sources informing the theology of this work)

Arnold, Eberhard. The Early Christians: In Their Own Words. Farmington, PA: Plough Publishing House, 1970.

Brown, Cynthia Stokes. "The Olympian Gods and Goddesses (Their Names & Powers)." July 19, 2023.

Cannon, Mae Elise. Social Justice Handbook: Small Steps for a Better World. Downers Grove, IL: IVP Books, 2009.

Corbett, Steve, and Brian Fikkert. When Helping Hurts: How to Alleviate Poverty Without Hurting the Poor and Yourself. Chicago: Moody Publishers, 2009.

DeSilva, David A. Honor, Patronage, Kinship, and Purity: Unlocking New Testament Culture. Downers Grove, IL: InterVarsity Press, 2000.

Dixon, Suzanne, ed. Childhood, Class, and Kin in the Roman World. New York: Routledge, 2001.

Dortzbach, Deborah, and Meredith W. Long. Blessing: The Story of Rwandan Churches Challenging the AIDS Crisis. World Relief Corporation, 2004.

Ellul, Jacques. Money and Power. Downers Grove, IL: InterVarsity Press, 1954.

Elmer, Duane. Cross-Cultural Servanthood: Serving the World in Christlike Humility. Downers Grove, IL: InterVarsity Press, 2006.

Engel, James F., and William A. Dyrness. Changing the Mind of Missions: Where Have We Gone Wrong? Downers Grove, IL: InterVarsity Press, 2000.

Finger, Reta Halteman. Of Widows and Means: Communal Meals in the Book of Acts. Grand Rapids, MI: Eerdmans, 2007.

Finney, Charles G. The Autobiography of Charles Finney. Old Tappan, NJ: Fleming H. Revell Company, 1908.

Guthrie, Stan. Missions in the Third Millennium. Waynesboro, GA: Paternoster Press, 2000.

Harrison, Lawrence E., and Samuel P. Huntington. Culture Matters: How Values Shape Human Progress. New York: Basic Books, 2000.

Herbert, Paul G. Transforming Worldviews: An Anthropological Understanding of How People Change. Grand Rapids, MI: Baker Books, 2008.

Hiebert, Paul G. Anthropological Reflections on Missiological Issues. Grand Rapids, MI: Baker Books, 1994.

Homer. The Iliad. Translated by Emily Wilson. New York: W. W. Norton & Company, 2003.

Josephus. The Jewish War. Translated by G. A. Williamson. New York: Penguin Books, 1959.

Katongole, Emmanuel, and Chris Rice. Reconciling All Things: A Christian Vision of Justice, Peace, and Healing. Downers Grove, IL: InterVarsity Press, 2008.

Keskin, Naci. Ephesus. Istanbul, Türkiye: Keskin Color Kartpostalcilik Ltd., 2006.

Lewis, C. S. God in the Dock. Grand Rapids, MI: Eerdmans, 2014.

Long, W. Meredith. Health, Healing, and the Kingdom of God: New Pathways to Christian Health Ministry in Africa. Waynesboro, GA: Regnum Books International, 2000.

Myers, Bryant L. Working with the Poor: New Insights and Learnings from Development Practitioners. Colorado Springs: Authentic Publishing, 1999.

Nouwen, Henri J. M. In the Name of Jesus: Reflections on Christian Leadership. New York: Crossroad, 1989.

Perkins, John M. Beyond Charity: The Call to Christian Community Development. Grand Rapids, MI: Baker Books, 1993.

Sachs, Jeffrey D. The End of Poverty: Economic Possibilities for Our Time. New York: Penguin Press, 2005.

Sire, James W. Naming the Elephant: Worldview as a Concept. Downers Grove, IL: InterVarsity Press, 2004.

Soerens, Matthew, and Jenny Hwang. Welcoming the Stranger: Justice, Compassion, and Truth in the Immigration Debate. Downers Grove, IL: InterVarsity Press, 2009.

Stark, Rodney. The Rise of Christianity: How the Obscure, Marginal Jesus Movement Became the Dominant Religious Force in the Western World in a Few Centuries. Princeton, NJ: Princeton University Press, 1996.

Tenney, Merrill C. New Testament Times. Grand Rapids, MI: Eerdmans, 1965.

Wohlleben, Peter. The Hidden Life of Trees: What They Feel, How They Communicate. Vancouver/Berkeley: Greystone Books, 2016.

Wright, N. T. Matthew for Everyone. Louisville, KY: Westminster John Knox Press, 2004.

Yunus, Muhammad. Banker to the Poor: Micro-Lending and the Battle Against World Poverty. New York: PublicAffairs, 1999.

Appendix

THE TITANS AND THE GODS OF OLYMPUS

Compiled by Cynthia Stokes Brown

We know the Greek origin story from the earliest Greek literary sources that have survived, Theogony and Works and Days, by Hesiod. This oral poem is thought to have been active sometime between 750 and 650 BCE, within decades of when the Homeric epics, The Iliad, and The Odyssey, took the form in which we know them. Archaeological findings support the creation story recorded in Hesiod's work; pottery from the eighth century BCE depicts the gods and goddesses he describes. Before Hesiod told this patriarchal version, in which the first woman is the cause of much trouble, Pandora, whose name means "gift giver," was known in oral tradition as a beneficent Earth goddess. In the beginning, there was Chaos, a yawning nothingness. Out of the void emerged Gaia (the Earth) and other divine beings—Eros (love), the Abyss (part of the underworld), and the Erebus (the unknowable place where death dwells). Gaia gave birth to Uranus (the sky) without male assistance, who then fertilized her.

From that union, the first Titans were born —six males: Coeus, Crius, Cronus, Hyperion, Iapetus, and Oceanus, and six females: Mnemosyne, Phoebe, Rhea, Theia, Themis, and Tethys. After Cronus (time) was born, Gaia and Uranus decreed that no more Titans would be born. Cronus castrated his father and threw the severed genitals into the sea, from which arose Aphrodite, goddess of love, beauty, and sexuality. Cronus became the ruler of the gods with his sister-wife, Rhea, as his consort. The other Titans became his court. Because Cronus had betrayed his father, he feared his offspring would do the same. So, each time Rhea gave birth, Cronus snatched up the child and ate it. Rhea hated this and tricked him by hiding one child, Zeus, and wrapping a stone in a baby's blanket so that Cronus ate the stone instead of the baby. When Zeus was grown, he fed his father a drugged drink, which caused Cronus to vomit, throwing up Rhea's other children and the stone. Zeus then challenged Cronus to go to war for the kingship of the gods. At last, Zeus and his siblings, the Olympians, were victorious, and the Titans were hurled down to imprisonment in the Abyss. The same concern plagued Zeus as his father, and after a prophecy that his first wife, Metis, would give birth to a god more extraordinary than he, he swallowed Metis. But she was already pregnant with Athena, and they both made him miserable until Athena, the goddess of wisdom, civilization, and justice, burst from his head — fully grown and dressed for war. Zeus could fight off all challenges to his power and remain the ruler of Mount Olympus, the home of the gods. One son of the Titans, Prometheus, did not fight with fellow Titans against Zeus and was spared imprisonment; he was given the task of creating man. Prometheus shaped man out of mud, and Athena breathed life into the clay figure. Prometheus made man stand upright as the gods did and gave him fire. Prometheus tricks Zeus, and to punish him, Zeus creates Pandora, the first woman of stunning beauty, wealth, and a deceptive heart and lying tongue. He also gave Pandora a box, which she was commanded never to open. Still, eventually, her curiosity got the best of her, and she opened the box to release all kinds of evil, plagues, sorrows, misfortunes, and hope at the bottom of the book.

ABOUT THE AUTHOR

Gary C. Fairchild has spent a lifetime serving the church and engaging with communities around the world. Alongside his wife, Connie, he has ministered as a pastor, missionary, and humanitarian worker in North America, Southeast Asia, Africa, and Latin America. His passion is to help people experience the transforming power of the Gospel in both personal faith and community life.

Gary writes with the conviction that the message of Jesus is as relevant today as it was in the first century. His reflections draw on Scripture, history, and stories from years of ministry, weaving together a vision of the Kingdom of God that renews lives and restores hope. When he is not writing, Gary enjoys time with his children, grandchildren, and is grateful to share life's journey with his beloved wife, Connie.

www.ingramcontent.com/pod-product-compliance
Lightning Source LLC
LaVergne TN
LVHW010647110826
845149LV00014B/2977

* 9 7 9 8 9 9 5 3 5 5 2 3 6 *